The
CODFISH
DREAM

David Giblin

The
CODFISH
DREAM

CHRONICLES OF A WEST COAST FISHING GUIDE

VICTORIA · VANCOUVER · CALGARY

Heritage House Publishing Company Ltd.
heritagehouse.ca

Cataloguing information available from Library and Archives Canada

978-1-77203-242-0 (pbk)
978-1-77203-243-7 (epub)

Edited by Kate Juniper
Proofread by Sarah Weber
Cover and interior design by Jacqui Thomas
Cover images by Alfiram/Dreamstime.com
Dedication page illustration by David Giblin

The interior of this book was produced on 100% post-consumer recycled paper,
processed chlorine free, and printed with vegetable-based inks.

We acknowledge the financial support of the Government of Canada through the
Canada Book Fund (CBF) and the Canada Council for the Arts, and the Province
of British Columbia through the British Columbia Arts Council and the Book
Publishing Tax Credit.

22 21 20 19 18 1 2 3 4 5

Printed in Canada

To Kim

CONTENTS

one THE CODFISH DREAM

HOME-STYLE COOKING, the neon sign said. I was very hungry, but something about the diner made me hesitate and stop just inside the doorway. Red vinyl-topped chrome stools, the kind you can spin around on, were tucked under a long Formica counter. Black menus in chrome holders matched the napkin dispensers and the shiny salt and vinegar containers. Each booth along one wall displayed a chrome and glass control for the Wurlitzer jukebox that squatted in the corner: three plays for a quarter. The place smelled of onions and the hot fat in the deep fryer. I could watch the cook put my order together. I got over my hesitation and took a seat at the counter. The restaurant was empty, except for the cook, and she didn't say anything to me, just kept polishing glasses with a white cloth. I picked up a menu. The specials were handwritten on a piece of paper taped inside: Salisbury steak or liver and onions, a choice of blueberry or cherry pie for desert. The soup of the day was navy bean. I was too hungry to think, so I ordered a deluxe burger with fries, and for ten cents extra I got mushrooms.

With one quick motion of the cook's hand, the patty hit the grill with a satisfying sizzle. The cook carefully opened the bun and placed it beside the patty. She hadn't said one word the whole time, and her silence was beginning to make me uncomfortable. But before I could think about it too long, the burger was ready. She slid it to me across the counter. It was fresh and juicy, with lettuce and tomatoes spilling onto a big side of fries. I picked it up with both hands and took a huge bite.

My mouth closed onto something sharp and metallic. A tremendous jerk from the burger lifted me right off the stool and up toward the ceiling. The diner disappeared and I found myself underwater being pulled toward the surface.

I tried to move my hands but couldn't make them work. I kicked my legs but they felt strange; looking down I saw they had changed to fins. I started to thrash about wildly. A dark shape loomed above me. As I was dragged closer I saw two people smiling down at me. One of them was holding something. The other looked like the cook from the diner. I didn't think they had my best interests in mind. I knew if they brought me to the surface it would mean my death.

I gave one last desperate shake of my head and woke up, sweating, in my bed.

two **HOMING**

IT WAS 1983 and I was approaching the summer of my thirty-second year. For some time, five years to be precise, it had been my habit to spend the summer months fishing the waters around Stuart Island, north of Vancouver, BC. It had become a popular place, especially among well-to-do American sportsmen. Luxury yachts belonging to members of the Seattle Yacht Club crowd the docks, and a steady stream of float planes come in and out daily.

Now, I don't mean to imply that I was one of these amateur anglers, or a dilettante chasing after various and elusive species of fish merely for sport. Nor do I want to give the impression that I was only (and here I must lower my voice to a whisper) a *tourist*. My reason for travelling to Stuart Island each summer originated from a more primitive need: that grim spectre money forced me to take employment there as a salmon fishing guide.

The alarming state of my bank balance announced the coming season. As the summer grew nearer, the sum of money left in my bank account grew smaller. Finally, I had to leave my home on the southern end of Vancouver Island and travel north to the small town of Campbell River. There I could purchase any groceries and supplies I needed and charter a float plane to take me the last few miles to my destination.

Campbell River is world famous for the salmon that return there each year. Its shops offer an abundance of items a fisherman might need: the latest advances in rods and reels, as well as hooks, lines, sinkers, nets, and other such goods. Fishing equipment is everywhere, even in the gas stations and drugstores. The whole town revolves around sport fishing. All its streets lead down to the water. A jetty reaches out over the waves along the shore. Scores of people line the railings. They drop a lure into the water below and try to catch one of the salmon as they swim past on their way to spawn in the river.

The streets fill with people, their eyes slightly vacant, their minds lost in fishing reveries. They spend hours inspecting the rods, reels, and lures. They talk endlessly about the fish they have caught, the fish they did not catch, the fish they want to catch. I was too busy for such distractions. These lost fisher-folk, wandering the sidewalks and cluttering the aisles of the stores while staring off into the distance, acted only as obstacles to my errands.

After spending a couple of days in town, it finally came time to appear at the float plane dock, early, for the flight to Stuart Island. After a strange and restless sleep, I left the motel room and made my way to the mouth of Campbell River and the float plane docks. There I would meet up with another guide, my roommate for the summer.

three VOP 1V0

WE HAD SHARED a small cottage for the last couple of seasons and so had developed a routine. Like me, my roommate began the season by spending a few days in town, running errands such as retrieving our outboard motors from the shop where they were stored for the winter. Usually we would have met on Stuart Island, but this year a few unavoidable changes had us flying in together.

A de Havilland Beaver on floats waited at the dock where our supplies, including the two motors, lay in a pile ready for loading. My roommate paced up and down beside them. His name was Ivor Vopnstrom. Vop was twenty-five years old or, as he preferred to say, on his twenty-fifth revolution around the sun. The postal code for Stuart Island is VOP 1V0. All the guides immediately nicknamed him Vop. I'd known him for two years before I ever discovered his real name.

Vop usually went out of his way to appear calm and collected, but that was not the case this morning. He hovered about, barely acknowledging my arrival, as the dock boys began loading the plane. His jaw muscles clenched and unclenched. His hands moved about his body, roaming in and out of pockets, straying behind his back, wandering from ear to buttonhole, never finding rest. At first I took this unease to betray concern over the equipment. A broken rod tip is a minor nuisance in town, but it becomes a major complication in a remote area like the one we were going to. Spare parts are not so easy to come by; a fifty-cent fuse that blows at the wrong time can cost hundreds of dollars in lost wages thanks to the trip to town for a replacement.

The engines were the last things loaded, and at two hundred pounds apiece the dock boys needed our help wrestling them up the steps and into the aircraft. Vop worked himself into a froth, grunting and straining, and even though it was a cold spring morning he was sweating profusely. Vop wasn't much for small talk, though he liked to get in the last word, and always offered his opinion about a more efficient way to do the task at hand. Yet this morning he remained strangely silent.

It occurred to me that I had never known him to go up in an airplane. In the past we had always arrived at the island by boat. Boat was the main means of transportation among all these islands, as common as a pickup truck in other parts of the world. Vop lived on an island to the south of Stuart Island, and he usually stored his boat and motors there. But this year he had been at university on the mainland all winter, and his motor had been in the shop with mine. His boat was at Stuart Island, so the only way for him to get there was to fly in. I was coming to the conclusion that Vop—Vop the unfazed—hated to fly.

When Vop finally did say something it was to offer to sit in the rear of the plane. The boat motors were balanced precariously back there between the seats, and he offered to steady them.

"We don't want them to fall over," he said, and smiled.

It was a smile of abject terror.

I enjoy flying. I'll sit up front any chance I get. I was only too happy to let him sit with the engines. He wedged himself into a seat beside the doorway. When I looked back from the co-pilot's seat, his arms were wrapped around the engines and his knuckles were already turning white. The flight to the island would be mercifully short, at least, a matter of some fifteen minutes. I settled in my seat. It was a clear, cloudless day, and I intended to enjoy the flight.

The float plane taxied out to the channel for takeoff. It first had to work its way past the sandbars at the river mouth. The pilot turned to me. He was a tragically dashing figure who might have been more at home in a Spitfire over the English Channel than in a dingy little float plane, flying from one dingy logging camp to another. He had to yell over the intense noise of the rotary engine. His accent sounded foreign.

"So, you want to go to Stuart Island?"

"I guess so," I yelled back, "although on a day like today it really doesn't matter where I end up."

"That's a mad place."

"What makes you say that?"

"Well, all those people there just mad to go fishing."

"Yeah, I guess they are." I was just trying to be agreeable.

"You must be mad, too."

"What makes you say that?"

"You're going there, aren't you?"

The plane turned into the ocean currents that swirled at the river mouth, and the sun shone through the window behind him. His head disappeared in the glare. Dark glasses hid his eyes. All I could see of him were his teeth as he smiled; I caught a glint of gold.

We reached the part of the waterway reserved for takeoff and landing, and the pilot turned his attention to the controls. He gave the engine full throttle and the nose of the aircraft rose steeply. There was a slight chop on the water, and we bounced a little as we picked up speed. I sat forward to see out the windshield. We had just become airborne when I felt something warm run down my leg.

I looked down at my feet. The bottom halves of my new white deck shoes disappeared into an inky blackness. My heart stopped. It was like peering into another dimension. If the floor of the plane had suddenly dropped away, leaving my feet dangling in space, I wouldn't have been any more shaken. Then I caught a whiff of hot oil and realized what must have happened.

On the console between the pilot and me was a filler cap for adding oil to the engine. The cap must have been loose, so as the nose of the plane rose on takeoff, oil had spilled out onto the floor.

Conversation inside an airborne Beaver is impossible. You can't yell hard enough to talk. I nudged the pilot with my elbow and pointed to the oil at my feet. He didn't seem all that concerned. Perhaps it was something that happened on a regular basis. He casually shrugged his shoulders, as if to suggest disdain for the maintenance people, and simply tightened the cap. He flashed me another gold-toothed smile and turned his attention back to flying.

The smell of hot oil filled the plane. It settled into the back and enveloped Vop like warm syrup. He began sniffing the air suspiciously. To his already strained mind the smell could only mean something was very wrong. A low moan made itself heard over the noise of the engine. I turned round to offer some sort of encouragement. Vop was staring about wildly, the fatted calf being led to the altar. His eyes rolled in their sockets. To be in the air was one thing; to be up in the air in a burning plane was clearly too much for him. He was beginning to crumble.

By this time we were over Quadra Island and starting our descent to Stuart Island. It would be time to land in a matter of minutes. The ordeal Vop was suffering would soon be over. However, as the pilot began the approach to the dock at our cottage, a large motor yacht was leaving the marina next door, trailing a huge wake behind it. It created a series of waves right in front of us. The pilot had no choice but to set the plane down regardless.

It hit the first wave and bounced back high in the air. The motor Vop was clinging to shifted and pushed him against the rear door. The plane bounced again as it hit the next wave. The door flew open and Vop, still clinging to the engine, was now dangling out the door feet first. He opened his eyes long enough to catch a view of water rushing past. The plane hit the next wave, and the spray from the impact soaked him from the knees down.

He couldn't get off the plane fast enough.

It dropped us at our dock and I tied the plane up. I stood in a small pool of slightly used, high-grade engine oil and watched as Vop heaved our things off the plane like a man possessed. He made a squishing sound with every step. As he worked he mumbled to himself. "I can get out of a car and walk. I can even get out of a boat and swim. But I'll be damned if I'll get out of a plane and bloody well fly." It would have been dangerous to get in his way.

He barely needed help getting the outboard engines down the steps and onto the dock. The plane emptied, we watched as it taxied back into the bay and took off. Vop was calmer after that. We carried the groceries up to the cottage.

Food always has a calming effect, so we opened up the boxes and found something for dinner. We celebrated our first night back on Stuart Island with a bottle of wine. Then we opened another one to celebrate getting back without being killed.

four **LOST CIVILIZATIONS**

YEARS AGO, BEFORE the Depression and the Second World War came along and changed things forever, the coast of British Columbia was more richly populated than it is now. Wherever there was shelter from the gales of winter, wherever the sun shone even in the darkest days, wherever natural clearings made the best site for an orchard, and wherever freshwater creeks ran clear and clean to the ocean, invariably someone has at one time erected a small but comfortable cottage. These cottages tend to share a similar floor plan and style of architecture. They have pantries and sheds attached to store wood and boats. They have deep front porches and they share the same curiously rounded windows. The tops of the windows arch, giving the rooms' interiors the feel of a church hall.

When these cottages were built, steamships served the coast from Vancouver to Prince Rupert. Many of the place names refer to the ships' presence. Stuart Island Resort, on the south end of the island, below the first set of rapids, is still called the Landing. A regular stop on the steamship's route, the ship would be forced to wait for the tide to turn in order to navigate the rapids during slack tide. Mail and supplies reached the islands on these ships, and people wishing to travel simply stepped onto the boat and stepped off again in Vancouver or anywhere else along the way.

Life must have been serene and satisfying. The coast was still abundant with fish, shellfish, grouse, and deer. Wild, edible plants and mushrooms grew everywhere, and the gardens of the homesteaders were prolific.

The Indigenous people here were unique among the world's civilizations. There was so much food that it allowed them the leisure time to develop a sophisticated art and culture. Remnants of their traps and weirs for harvesting salmon, placed in the mouths of the creeks, remained around Stuart Island.

After the war, life was so disrupted that it never returned to its former ways. The old steamships were retired, and the homes and cottages entered into a period of neglect.

The place Vop and I shared was one of these cottages. It must have been beautiful once, but years of long, wet winters had had their effect. The incessant damp had wrinkled the whole building, like skin kept too long in a bathtub. The siding was cracked and warped; the paint was peeling. In spots the wood showed through and was bleached to a silver colour by the weather. The roof was disappearing beneath a layer of moss that insulated the interior and was the only thing that kept out the rain. Now the cottage didn't seem to have been built so much as grown in the clearing like a toadstool, a strange, elaborate, and rather large one, complete with round-topped windows and plumbing.

Inside mildew bloomed gloriously across the ceiling, watermarks stained the curling wallpaper, and the kitchen linoleum was as rippled as the ocean outside. In the absence of human beings, obscure species of bugs had taken over. Spiders had lived here so long they had developed an advanced spider civilization that had then gone into decline. The remains of their webs spread out from the corners of the ceiling like the ruins of ancient temples. The corners of the house were full of creepings and scurryings; the mice in the back rooms could be heard playing cards.

The landlord used the cottage as storage space during the off season. It was filled with all the odds and ends needed to support human life on this part of the planet toward the end of the twentieth century. Rust fell in huge flakes off the boom chains on the floor. One-hundred-gallon propane tanks left rust-red rings on the green shag rug in the living room. An old barbecue corroded peacefully next to a huge cardboard box full of old outboard parts that was forever moved from one place to another on the chance that one day the contents would prove useful.

After the flight and the two bottles of wine, we were past caring about the conditions. Our dinner was eaten like a picnic amid the rubble of an archeological dig. We cleared enough space to drop our belongings, chased most of the bugs out of the bedrooms, and passed out for the night.

Vop woke up before me in the morning. I heard him get out of bed, open his bedroom door, and make his way into the kitchen. Then there was a long silence. I got out of bed to investigate. When I entered the kitchen, I found him standing in the middle of the floor amid all the chaos and clutter, wearing his bright yellow bathrobe and staring down at one of the boxes we had brought in the night before. I threaded my way through all the junk and came up beside him. He wore the look of a prison inmate waking up after a long and pleasant dream only to find he was still in prison.

A shaft of early morning sunlight shone through the kitchen window onto the box by his foot. Warming herself on top of the box, a piece of Vop's favourite cheese in her paws, was a very small mouse. She stared back up at Vop, her little whiskers gleaming in the sun. She was no more afraid of him than she was of one of the propane tanks. She nibbled the cheese with the distracted air of someone enjoying popcorn during the good part of a movie. When I disturbed the scene, she hopped delicately off the box and disappeared in the maze of boxes around us.

Over the years Vop spent much time and energy reclaiming this cottage, and others like it on other islands. There were times when the futility of it all was brought home to him.

five **THE ORANGE ORIFICE**

THE REST OF the day we spent cleaning house. We began by moving the heavy equipment out of the living room. The boom chains would be needed for the landlord's float house when it arrived, so we took them down to the dock, along with the propane tanks that would be filled when the fuel barge came by in a few days. We moved the barbecue out to its spot on the lawn, ready for summer cookouts. The box full of outboard parts was moved once more (you never know when those parts might come in handy) into the boatshed at the side of the house.

The boom chains and propane tanks had bled rust stains into the rug all winter, leaving a curious abstract pattern similar to the pattern on the living room curtains. After a short discussion we decided to leave the stains where they were— a decorating decision influenced by the impossibility of ever successfully removing them. The curtains and most of the other furnishings were remnants of an unfortunate redecoration that had taken place some time in the fifties. A rising affluence had given people the leisure time to rediscover places like Stuart Island and use the buildings for summer homes and fishing lodges.

The signs of a fifties aesthetic were everywhere. The kitchen was done in a grey, metal-flake Formica. The counter was covered with it, the edges finished in chrome. The kitchen table had a grey Formica top with chrome legs and matching chairs covered in grey vinyl. In the living room, to complement the curtains and the green shag, sat a square and uncomfortable looking couch and matching chair covered in a brown nubbly material. The coffee table had the same sharp-edged look, the fifties' idea of future furniture. Walking into the house was like entering a poorly maintained museum exhibit.

Next to the side entrance, which opened out onto the lawn, was a built-in bookcase. Like another exhibit in the same museum, it held a large collection of yellowing paperbacks from the same period as the decor. I had read all of them over the summers I had lived in the house, but they were classics— the original Alfred Hitchcock mystery collections, to name a few—and could be returned to time and time again.

By late afternoon we had the place almost livable. There was a fire going in the wood stove, which didn't smoke too badly. Dinner was cooking on the gas range in the kitchen. I was on the couch reading a murder mystery when Vop announced he was going to have a shower. Vop took his personal hygiene very seriously. Wearing his yellow mono-grammed bathrobe, he advanced on the bathroom with the gravity of a bishop in a religious procession.

Actually, to call the bathroom a room was glorifying it. When the house was first built, an indoor toilet was considered rather effete. The room Vop was about to enter was a later addition, designed by people who had developed a taste for modern conveniences. It was added, no doubt, during the redecoration in an attempt to mimic the creature comforts found in the city. No bathing in creeks or using an outhouse for these newcomers.

The bathroom was not much more than a lean-to tacked onto the side of the cottage. It contained a toilet, a sink, a metal shower stall, and a propane-fired hot water tank that took up most of the room's available space. The landlord had been by to light the hot water tank a couple of days before we had arrived, but we had completely forgotten to include the bathroom in our cleaning frenzy.

When Vop entered he found that the spiders had saved their most important temples for this forgotten room. Egg sacks containing members of their paramount bloodlines had been stored here, and the shower stall had been used like a sacrificial well: the husks of victims lay thickly on its floor. Water, which had been left running to prevent the pipes from freezing over in winter, had seeped from the faucets for so long that spawning green algae mingled with the dead flies. Mildew grew up the metal walls, and here and there was the shocking orange accent of a small fungus known as wood ear.

The recently lit water heater had added a moist warmth to the room that allowed the rich fungal odours to reach their full bouquet. When Vop opened the door and entered the cramped space, the thick atmosphere caught him by surprise. Instinctively, he reached out and drew back the shower curtain. The shock of so much unexpected life and death hit Vop full in the chest. His reflexive gasp caused him to inhale more of the fetid air.

From my position on the couch I heard a thin, strangled cry—a cry that coincided so nicely with my choice of reading material that at first I thought it was in my own head. Then a stream of profanities issued from the bathroom, followed by a desperate, scrabbling sound as Vop tried to close the curtain on the awful sight. No doubt the delicate little mushrooms curled up in embarrassment.

Vop stalked past me and out of the house, and I soon heard him enter the boatshed. There was a great clattering as he dug through the cans of paint stored there. In a few moments he reappeared, armed with a long-handled scrub brush, a paintbrush, and a can of paint. I recognized the paint. It was the same stuff he had used on the hull of his fibreglass boat: a lurid, throbbing orange that was the product of a miss-mixed batch. The salesman had given him a great deal on it.

The shower stall thumped and rumbled as Vop scrubbed it clean. He then applied a thick coat of paint to the metal walls, sealing in anything the scrub brush had missed. It gave a lumpy, organic quality to the finished look.

When Troutbreath saw it for the first time he shuddered and said, "Huh, it looks just like an orifice."

six **THE HERBY DERBY**

AT THE SAME time as Vop was standing in a room full of rusting hardware and useless engine parts looking down at a mouse eating cheese, Herbert Crane was standing in a room full of leather furniture and high-end Japanese electronic equipment looking down at his son eating a cheese bagel. Herbert had looked down at his son one day not long before and realized the boy was no longer six years old. The child of six had called him Daddy; they had played ball together, rolled around on the front lawn, and hugged each other. To reach out and hug his son now would be acutely embarrassing for both of them.

Herbert didn't know exactly when this change had taken place, but he also couldn't remember the last time they'd had a real conversation. It was almost as if he was dealing with a complete stranger. They ate together, lived under the same roof, watched the game on TV, but, he realized, he didn't know anything about this person who was his son.

From the spot in which Herbert was standing he could see out the front window of his house. A broad expanse of lush grass sloped down to the edge of Lake Washington. Tied to an expensive set of docks were a very expensive luxury yacht and a brand new Cessna 185 on floats. Its propeller blades gleamed in the morning sun.

Seeing his belongings arrayed before him usually filled him with an overwhelming pride—not a selfish pride, but a pride all tied up in feelings about the country he lived in. It was a country that allowed people to achieve and aspire, and had allowed him to ultimately become vastly successful with only a small starter loan of some $500,000 from his father. It was the kind of pride that asked him, or rather *demanded* of him, that he share his success with others who hadn't had the same opportunities. He liked the fact that his country tried to help other, less fortunate countries with foreign aid; that was the way it should be, like from father to a grateful son. In his own small way he was able to do the same thing: to help people in other, less fortunate places aspire to more and achieve better. It made him happy to do that. Looking down at the dock today, though, he could only think about the one person with whom he hadn't been able to share this largesse. He could only think about his son.

Two years ago, during an especially expansive moment, he and a neighbour on the lake had helped their favourite guide at Stuart Island buy a small and very rustic resort there. He put a few trips a year through the lodge, mainly business associates, clients, and people that worked for his company. The resort wasn't there to make money for him; he just genuinely liked the guide who was now his partner, and it was something he'd wanted to do for him.

Of course, it also fulfilled some rustic fantasy. The log cabins, the trophy-mounted animals in the main lodge . . . it was like a shrine to the outdoors, a symbol of manly activity—or at least Herbert's idea of such things. Herbert liked to think of himself as an outdoorsman. He was a member of the Seattle Yacht Club. He water-skied, went sport fishing, and operated his own boat and plane. He owned shares in Eddie Bauer.

As he stood there looking down at the float plane and thinking about the lodge up there in Canada, a plan took shape in his mind. The best way for he and his son to get reacquainted was to spend a few days together at the lodge. He could picture it in his mind already. The regular guests wouldn't start arriving for a few days yet. They would have the whole resort to themselves. The fishing would be great, and there was always work to be done this time of the year. Nothing like a little backwoods adventure to achieve some healthy male bonding!

Getting up early and going fishing, maybe chopping wood or building something with their hands.

Of course, Herbert had never built anything with his hands in his life, but his mounting enthusiasm allowed him to overlook such small details. He wanted do to something simple and life affirming. He knew they could do with some help up there. They'd be happy to have him and his son. Herbert smiled as he stood in the window, that old feeling of pride flooding back. Yes, he just knew this was going to work out fine.

Once Herbert had made up his mind he acted on it. That was the way he was. It was how he had taken that small loan from his father and built the company he had today. Regardless of his son's protestations, he would fly them up there this very morning. It was only a two-hour flight in the new plane. They could get up there in time for lunch, even with going through customs. He was taking some time off work anyway. They could get by without him for a few days.

His wife got that odd little smile of hers, the smile that reminded him of that famous painting by the Italian guy. She wished him luck. It wasn't until he was in the plane and flying north that he wondered what, exactly, she had meant by that.

He didn't think about it too much, though, what with the prospect of the days ahead. He hadn't spent much time at the resort since he had bought the place, a terrible oversight. It was all part of the problem driving the wedge between him and his son—he had gotten too caught up in the minutiae of running a large, successful business. He let it consume too much of his time, too many of his thoughts. It was time to step back and take stock of the situation.

He thought about his wife again. That odd, enigmatic smile she had given him as he was getting ready to leave stayed with him. Perhaps he wasn't spending enough time with her, either. Certainly there wasn't the gap that existed between him and his son, but there was something in that smile and he couldn't quite put his finger on it. Maybe she would enjoy some time at the lodge as well, kind of a family thing. He hummed to himself as he guided the plane north, already thinking about the times they would share there.

In the excitement of leaving so spontaneously for the island, one small detail was overlooked. It was a minor thing, really, a gesture of good manners. No one had remembered to radio the lodge and tell them they were coming.

They showed up shortly before lunch. Nelson, the guide and Herbert's partner, was sitting down to eat when he saw a plane make a rough, bumpy landing and then taxi toward the resort. Nelson didn't recognize the brand new plane, but there was something familiar in the way it was being mishandled. Nelson recalled hearing that Herbert had recently taken delivery of a new Cessna. A sense of foreboding grew in him. He left his lunch and went down to the dock.

Herbert and his son were tying the plane up when Nelson arrived. The two of them stood up and smiled at him as he approached. Seeing them there, with the plane tied to the dock and the islands behind them, reminded Nelson of something he had seen before. He tried to place the image, and then it came to him: they looked like something out of one of those outdoor clothing catalogues people kept leaving around the lodge. The photos in them showed guys with perfectly blow-dried hair standing around a dock or an incredibly neat campsite. They were always smiling, as though one of them had just said something terribly amusing. The people in the photos looked too clean to have ever been anywhere near the outdoors. Nobody Nelson knew would ever wear clothes like that around a campsite. The only time Nelson ever got that dressed up was when he was going to dinner with his wife's parents.

There was something else about those photos. The men always wore small leather cases attached to their belts, meant to contain some sort of folding knife. Herbert had one on his belt. Many of the guests, especially the ones who made the most noise about being the outdoor type, wore ones just like it. The curious thing was, in all the years Nelson had taken them out fishing with their little knife cases, he had never seen a knife outside its case, let alone used.

Herbert reached out and shook Nelson's hand enthusiastically. He announced that he and his son were there to help.

They wanted to do whatever needed doing to get the resort ready for the coming season. He knew how much work the place needed, and they were just here to be of assistance. No matter how dull or dirty the job, they were Nelson's men. Nelson was appalled.

They joined Nelson for lunch. While Herbert chatted on happily about his plans for the future, Nelson ate his meal in silence. He tried to think of something that the two of them could do without getting in the way. Herbert was right about one thing: there was a huge amount of work to finish before the first guests were due to arrive. Nelson finally decided to send them out to cut firewood. It was one of those little chores that he never seemed to find the time for. It was necessary; the main lodge and all the cabins had fireplaces, and it was still cold and damp this time of year. And they would be out of the way. The activity was manly enough, and Herbert could feel as if he was contributing to the comfort of the guests. They could arm themselves with mauls and splitting wedges, axes and chainsaws. Herbert might even get some chain oil on that new chamois cloth shirt he was wearing.

Nelson had to laugh. When he needed outdoor clothing he went to the thrift shop in Campbell River. His latest find had been a dozen surplus postal uniforms. They were of high quality wool and cotton and still had the shoulder badges and postal markings attached. He felt they lent an air of gravitas— the full weight of a federal institution—to any work he did around the resort.

After lunch Herbert and his son set off to cut firewood. Nelson had given them explicit instructions. There was a gigantic Douglas fir log lying on the beach in front of the resort. Its huge size and freshly cut appearance suggested it had broken away from a passing log boom. Nelson had found it floating and towed it back to the lodge with the workboat.

"I'd leave that fir for now," Nelson had warned them. "The tide is on the way in and that log will soon be afloat. I've dogged it off to a tree down there so it's in no danger of floating away. I'd start on the alder up on the hill."

Nelson didn't mention he thought the alder was more their speed. He had some concerns about Herbert's expertise with a chainsaw, and bucking up a log that big was not for a beginner.

The main lodge buildings sat on the top of a large rock outcropping almost surrounded by water at high tide. A path led from the lodge to a walkway that joined it to the main island and continued along the shoreline, giving access to the workshops, boatshed, and other guest cabins that perched on the edge of the dense forest. The shore was very rocky, and the land rose steeply behind the cabins to become a rugged tree-covered mountain that loomed over the resort.

Having armed themselves with as much hardware as they could carry, Herbert and his son tottered off down the path from the lodge. It was a beautiful spring day, and they stopped to admire an eagle in a tall snag. The bird's high-pitched, wickering cry echoed around them.

"Isn't that a magnificent creature?"

Herbert marvelled at the sight of the bird. Its form evoked his feelings toward his country in a way he could never explain. Eagles were America for him. He felt good every time he saw one, which around Seattle was extremely rarely. He was glad to see that they were a common sight around his resort.

The fir log lay on the rocks below the generator shed where the walkway began. It was a massive piece of wood, about four feet through at the butt and over thirty feet long. It was supported at either end by large boulders. One round cut from this log would split up into several days' firewood for the whole resort. It seemed to Herbert that the tide still had quite a way to come before it posed a problem. He carried with him a brand new STIHL chainsaw. Nelson had just bought it for the resort, and Herbert had talked him into letting him use it. With a saw like this a man could do some work! He could whip a couple of rounds off that log in the time it took to think about it.

Herbert's son had his misgivings but was quickly overruled, and additionally received a lecture on the importance of seizing the moment and making tough, executive decisions on one's own initiative. Herbert started the chainsaw. He walked up to the middle of the log and, looking the picture of executive confidence, started his first cut.

"But Dad"—Herbert's son had to make himself heard over the noise of the generator as well as the chainsaw—"shouldn't you at least start at one end of the log?"

Herbert had disappeared in a blizzard of wood chips as the new saw blade ripped easily into the log. His son's concerns were drowned out by the noise. The smell of freshly cut fir filled the air and Herbert breathed it in happily. This was what it was all about.

"Hey, Dad."

The son tried again, but Herbert was enjoying himself too much to pay attention, even if he could hear him.

Now, as most people that do much woodcutting are aware, Herbert was ignoring not only his son but a certain law of physics as well. A log suspended in the middle sags, from the force of gravity, and as the log is sawn, the cut closes up on itself. A log this big closes so tightly about whatever is in there that it becomes a part of the log. Herbert was almost a third of the way into the log when it happened.

The engine stalled and Herbert tried to remove the chainsaw from the log to see what was the matter, but the saw wouldn't budge. He tried to wriggle it free, but he may as well have been wriggling a tree branch with the name STIHL painted on the side.

Herbert was red faced and breathing hard when he finally faced the futility of trying to free the blade. The tide was also becoming a problem.

A huge volume of water, moving through a maze of channels and around so many small islands, doesn't flow in a steady stream. Sometimes it hangs back and then comes in with a rush. It fills the channels in a series of surges and can rise two or three feet in a matter of minutes. Herbert was so intent on the jammed saw that he forgot about the tide. It was his son who brought it up.

"Ummm...Dad." Now that he only had to compete against the sound of the generator it was easier for him to make himself heard. "Hey . . . Dad, I think the tide's coming in faster than you expected."

The water was already starting to lap at Herbert's feet. It would soon be high enough to float the log. The chainsaw was in danger of being soaked in the salt water, and even Herbert knew what salt water could do to an engine.

Nelson was on the roof of the lodge repairing some shingles that had loosened in a winter storm. He heard an embarrassed clearing of the throat below him.

"Ummm . . . my dad sent me to find you. He's got a little problem."

Nelson peered over the edge of the roof; Herbert's son smiled awkwardly back up at him. By the time Nelson had climbed down off the roof, walked out along the boardwalk to the workshop, collected another chainsaw, and walked back, the tide had gained on them even more.

The only way to save the trapped saw was to cut down at an angle and remove wedge-shaped pieces of wood from around the trapped blade. Once you expose the saw you must open the cut with carefully placed faller's wedges, specially made from nylon, so as not to damage the blade. It would be slow, tiring work made even worse by the water.

The tide continued to rise, and before long Nelson was splashing around up to his waist in the icy water. Herbert offered encouragement from a dry vantage point. The job became more difficult as the log began to float. It rocked and twisted around as he worked. Nelson thrashed about in the water, swearing to himself, trying to ignore the numbing cold. The saw eventually came loose and escaped any serious damage, but Nelson was completely soaked and chilled to the bone. He headed back to the lodge to warm up and change into some dry clothing.

Herbert and his son stayed with the chainsaws and other equipment piled on the walkway. Herbert felt bad for all the trouble he had caused Nelson, and for taking him away from his work. He wanted to make it up to him. Besides, Herbert hadn't got where he was in the world by being a quitter—if anything, a little adversity only made him more determined to succeed. He remembered there was still that alder farther up the hillside.

Herbert grabbed the STIHL and told his son to follow. The trail to the wood started behind the generator shed. It led to a small clearing not more than fifty yards up the hill. Herbert marched into the clearing with determination. The alder lay amid a tangle of salal bushes, tree roots, and ferns. It was cut into lengths of ten or twelve feet, all no more than a foot thick. After a massive chunk like the fir this stuff resembled so many matchsticks. Herbert started up the chainsaw with renewed confidence.

Nelson had just finished changing and was finally starting to get warm. Even in the middle of summer the water was still ice cold. Twenty minutes immersed in the water was enough to cause death from hypothermia; Nelson was sure he had been wrestling with the saw for more than half an hour. Wrapped up in a thick wool blanket, he stood in the sunshine that streamed in the front windows and sipped some hot, fortified coffee. He looked down the trail to the lodge and saw Herbert's son approaching. Nelson was already putting his boots on when the boy opened the door.

"Ummm . . . Nelson, Dad hit something with the chainsaw up there on the hill and there's water spraying all over the place."

Herbert's first cut had not only sawn clean through a small alder log but kept on going through a three-inch-thick black hose he hadn't noticed lying beside the log. It was the water supply line, carrying the entire water supply for all the systems at the resort. The reservoir above was rapidly emptying itself onto the ground in the clearing. It had been a dry spring and water was a precious commodity. Nelson waded into the spraying water and was soaked once more. He took a moment to examine the extent of the damage. The line was sawn almost in two, and water was squirting out of the cut like a fountain. Nelson went off on another hike out to the workshop to gather the tools and fittings he would need.

He had to leave the two visitors alone while he did so. He made Herbert promise solemnly that he would not start another chainsaw. He made him look him in the eye and repeat the promise.

Herbert was really upset with himself. No matter how hard he tried, he only made more work for Nelson. He also wasn't making much of an impression on his son. He had no intention of starting a chainsaw, but perhaps there was something else he could do that would move things along. As he looked around the clearing an idea came to him. If he and his son could move the logs out of Nelson's way, he would have more room to work on the waterline. It was only a matter of flipping the logs end over end. They were so small Herbert and his son could manage quite easily to flip them down the hill toward the walkway. The logs would end up out of the way and closer to the woodshed.

He had his son help with the first log. They lifted it with ease and let go. The log fell down the hill and made a satisfying crash into the salal bushes. This might be fun. They picked up another and pushed it down the hill. This time it went farther and made a louder and even more satisfying crash. They set to the task with enthusiasm. Herbert and his son were enjoying themselves. They were finally doing something together, laughing and whooping each time another log crashed to the ground. They moved the logs end over end down the hill until they were in sight of the generator shed. A few more flips and the logs would be right next to the walkway.

On his way back from the workshop, Nelson was just rounding the last curve of the walkway when something made him look up. Herbert and his son were standing hip deep in the salal bushes just behind the generator shed. Red faced and smiling, they were balancing an alder log on its end. It looked as if they were about to let go of the log. Nelson saw what was about to happen.

It was as if time slowed for Nelson. He waved his hands, full of hose clamps and hose fittings, over his head. His mouth worked but his brain was too stunned to form words properly. The two on the hillside saw him waving. At that moment they had found a new joy in being together and wanted to share it with everyone. They waved back. Herbert was calling his son by his first name, Gary. They had formed a new father-and-son bond through the hard work and team effort of moving the logs. Nelson's waving just made them feel that much better about what they had accomplished. It was like an affirmation of their worthwhile achievements. They let the log fall.

It moved slowly at first, and then the law of gravity asserted itself. The log picked up speed, arching gracefully through the air. Nelson stood witness, his hands raised stupidly over his head. The log came crashing down. It landed on top of the main power line that carried electricity from the generator to the lodge and the rest of the cabins, as well as the workshop and the boatshed. There was a bright blue flash. The emergency shut-off switch stopped the generator and, as the diesel engine whined to a stop, a profound silence settled over the scene.

People always assume that being out in the country means being out in pure silence, but this is seldom the case. There are always the sounds of motors—chainsaw motors, outboard motors, airplane motors as they take off and land; and always there is the ever-present throb of generators. Either diesel- or gasoline-powered, they are always working anywhere you find people. The sounds are so common that you begin to take them for granted. You tune them out and they become part of the background.

When the generator shut down, it was as though Nelson was hearing silence for the first time.

Nelson very slowly brought his hands back down from their position over his head. They were filled with objects—hose clamps, fittings—and for a few seconds he stared at them. He had forgotten why he had them clutched in both hands.

He looked up to the hillside above him. Two people stood in the salal, smiling down at him. He nodded numbly as one of them spoke. The man's voice boomed out unnaturally in the silence. "Oh jeez," he said, so friendly. "Hey, don't worry about that, Gary and I will help you fix it."

seven **THE FAMILIAR**

HAVING A BOAT in the water at Stuart Island is not like having a car on the road in the city. There is a complex and subtle relationship between the boat and the owner that goes far beyond transportation or even status.

Seen from a distance, the guide boat is instantly recognizable. An experienced observer can watch a fishing hole from a mile or more away and, from the size, shape, and colour of the boats, know exactly who's there and even how good the fishing might be. The presence or absence of certain people and their boats speaks volumes about the kind of fishing taking place.

The interior of a boat takes on the personality of the owner and expresses the way they fish, their habits, and their outlook on life. Even to the uninitiated, certain things are obvious. Some guides are extremely efficient and organized, while others are unbelievably sloppy. A guide can take one look inside a boat and tell where the person was fishing, what kind of bait they were using, and other useful information just as easily as reading a newspaper.

The hours spent fishing in the back eddies, where you must be sensitive to the slightest nuance of the water as it surges around the boat, attunes a guide so closely to his boat that it becomes an extension of the body. Like a sea-faring centaur, a guide becomes half man, half boat. He turns and manoeuvres his craft as you might move your hand or your foot, seemingly without thinking or making a conscious decision. If you have to think about where your boat should be when you are in the rapids, then you have already lost control.

As Vop and I eased our boats into the water after the work of painting them and replacing the seats and motors, we weren't just gaining access to the fishing holes; we were regaining a part of our identity.

Once my boat is back in the water, the first thing I usually do is visit the resort run by my friend Nelson. He and his wife also run the only post office in the area. A visit to Nelson's place is a ritual played out by all the guides in the area, where they can change their address for the summer and say hello.

I found Nelson at the side of his generator shed, perched on the top of a ladder. The generator was shut down and he was absorbed in the task of splicing wires together.

"I thought you rewired the generator at the end of last season," I said.

Like most of the guides, Nelson didn't really enjoy shore work and he was a little sullen.

"I did, but Herbert and his son, Gary, are up for a visit. You can probably figure out the rest for yourself."

"What did he do this time?"

Nelson let out a deep sigh. He came down from the ladder and told me the whole story. He seemed relieved to be able to talk about it. Then he added, "This might even be funny except I got a call this morning." Nelson's life was seldom very simple. "There's a yacht on its way, due in by noon tomorrow. They want to go fishing as soon as they arrive. There's no way I'm going to finish all the stuff I've got to do. Do you think you could take them out for me?"

"Well, yeah, my boat is ready to go right now." A little extra work this time of year was always welcome.

"There's only one small catch."

"There's always a catch."

"Yeah, it's your old friend Morris Goldfarb."

eight MORRIS GOLDFARB

I HAD TAKEN Morris Goldfarb fishing before. Last summer Morris arrived during a particularly hot period of fishing. People were catching fish on every tide, and a number of big spring salmon over thirty pounds were already weighed in at the lodge. Fish that big are called *tyee*, a word used by the local Indigenous people that means "a damn big fish," or something to that effect. You could feel the excitement in the air; everyone, guides included, wanted to catch the next tyee. Along with the thrill of playing and landing such a large and powerful salmon on the light tackle we used, there was a certain status involved. Some people spent years and thousands of dollars without ever coming close to catching one. Having the experience put you in a select club. The resorts awarded prizes, special sweatshirts, and commemorative pins. Bottles of expensive champagne got popped open, and the guide responsible might be tipped hundreds of dollars. Over the course of the whole summer, during hundreds of hours of fishing, a guide might experience a tyee celebration only two or three times. Each time a guide dropped a piece of bait in the water he did it with great care; it might be the one that caught the next tyee.

Morris, however, couldn't have cared less. I don't think he even knew what a tyee was. A speech he had to give at a business meeting the following week commanded all of his attention. He had come to Stuart Island to relax and memorize his presentation. Somehow he found being out in the rapids in the middle of a busy fishing hole helped his concentration. He sat in the boat, rod jammed between his knees, the speech open on his lap, mumbling to himself as he memorized his lines. If I wanted him to let some more line out or reel in to check his bait, first I had to get his attention. Each time he turned to his speech he was transported out of my boat to a podium somewhere, holding an audience of his business peers enthralled with his insight and wit. For Morris this prospect was an experience far above any mere fishing action.

To make matters worse for me, every time a fish was caught near us I had to watch the lucky fisherman play his catch around the hole or out into the tide. There was no point trying to fish seriously; that took a certain amount of team-work and co-operation. We were fishing a spot known as the Second Hole, a large back eddy that moved the boats around it as though they were on a giant carousel. The main current flowed down the centre of the channel. The water it displaced pushed up against the shores of Stuart Island in a sweeping, circular fashion. The guides would line up at the top of the cir-cle, ride the faster water down the outside edge, head the bow of their boats in to the shore, and ride the slower moving back currents to the top of the hole again. We would have to watch the depth as we circled in order to avoid the rocks and reefs on the bottom. The salmon hid among these rocky places and waited for their food to come to them.

Morris, lost in his speech, couldn't be interrupted. I hung around near the top of the back eddy so as not to interfere with any of the more serious fishermen. The part of the hole we were at collected a great deal of driftwood and debris. It kept bumping into the line where it entered the water. At one point my line touched a small piece of bark. At the same time, the rod tip twitched, then dipped toward the water. Morris paid no attention and continued to mumble to himself. I asked him to reel in his line.

"Why?" he asked. "Do you think I need to?"

"Well, I think you might have a fish on. If you reel up, we'll find out."

"I don't feel anything there. Wasn't it just the line bumping into that piece of wood?"

Morris didn't want to bother with the interruption.

"Morris, as a favour to me, just reel up and see what happens."

"Are you sure? There's nothing there. I can't feel a thing. If a fish was there, I'd be able to feel it, wouldn't I? It was only that piece of wood."

Morris was growing impatient with me. I tried a different approach.

"Look, Morris, it's about time we changed bait anyway. Just bring the line in for me."

Morris sighed; he was a man beset by unreasonable people always making unreasonable demands on his time and patience.

"I really think it was only that piece of wood. The bait should still be okay, shouldn't it? The wood couldn't hit the bait, could it?"

We had been dragging the same herring around for at least an hour. It surprised me a fish would even bite it. Yet, from the way the line was acting, there was definitely something there. *Probably just a rock cod*, I thought.

Morris put down his papers on the empty seat next to him and started to reel the line in. He had turned the handle three or four times when the line suddenly started to peel off in the other direction. Morris clucked in exasperation.

"How the hell am I supposed to get the line in if the reel isn't working properly?" He gave me a dark stare as if the problem were my faulty equipment. The line was leaving his reel by now at an alarming pace.

"It's supposed to do that, Morris. You've got a fish on."

He still regarded me with suspicion, but the line was now making the reel scream as it left. It was a salmon all right, and judging by the way the line was running, it was a big one. I gunned the engine to follow the fish as it left the top of the hole. I convinced Morris that we had a salmon, but he was growing alarmed at the speed with which the line was leaving the reel.

"It's taking all my line, it's taking all my line," he wailed, and pawed at the reel.

"It's all right, Morris, you've got to let the fish run and take the line. You don't need to touch the reel."

I was coming down on a pack of guide boats as I followed the line that was knifing through the water. These were the same boats I had tried so hard to stay away from earlier. Now playing a big fish gave me the right of way. The other boats were getting out of the way for me. One was already bringing his lines into his boat, and I saw Wet Lenny cut his off with his fish knife. The salmon torpedoed out of the back eddy and went into the main current. There at least I didn't have the other boats to worry about, but the water was running at the peak of the tide. We were quickly in the middle of a vortex of swirling whitewater. Whirlpools were opening up all around us, and the fish was dragging us into the worst of them.

"It's taking all my line! Is the drag too loose, is the drag too loose?"

Morris kept up a constant wail as I steered the boat around the boiling water in front of us. His hand went to the reel again, and he began fiddling with the star wheel that sets the tension on the line.

"Don't touch that, Morris," I yelled over the roar of the water. "You'll break the damn fish off."

"My drag is too loose, my drag is too loose! It's taking all my line."

A note of panic was creeping into his voice.

"The drag is just fine, Morris, you've got plenty of line, let the fish run. You can't stop it."

I couldn't help myself. When my guests get themselves worked up into such a tizzy, I find I start adopting a tone of voice normally used on small children. I managed to get him to let go of the drag wheel, but I had given him something else to fret about.

"I touched the drag, I touched the drag. Did I tighten it? Is it too tight? Maybe I'll break the fish off."

I was too busy getting around a large whirlpool that had opened up in front of us. Morris was on his own until I could get the boat to calmer water. I steered us toward shore, away from the main current and into a quieter back eddy. I dragged the line behind me, hoping the fish would follow. When I was finally able to leave my seat Morris was carrying on a vicious argument with himself.

"Did I set the drag too tight, is it too tight? The line is still going out though, maybe it's too loose, maybe it's still too loose. I don't want to lose all my line..."

He didn't even notice me approach. I put my mouth right next to his ear and said very quietly, "Hey, Morris, shut the fuck up."

Morris never heard people talk to him like that. I got his attention immediately. He looked at me as if he'd just noticed there was someone else in the boat with him.

"Now," I said, looking him in the eye, "I want you to take a deep breath and count to ten."

Morris took a deep breath and counted to ten.

"Okay, I want you to start reeling the line in."

Without another word, Morris started to reel the line in. The salmon had stripped off more than half the line on the reel, so Morris had a job of cranking before him. I steered the boat to follow the line as it came out of the water; Morris only had to reel in the slack.

Quietly, in a robot-like fashion, Morris turned the handle of the reel. The salmon was coming to the surface and the line came in easily. A huge streamlined form began to take shape beneath my boat. It looked like a submarine coming to the surface.

The exhausted fish lay on its side and I was able to slip the net over its head. I needed to grab the hoop of the net with both hands to heave the fish into the boat. Seeing it laid out on the floor, I realized just how big it really was. The fish was a tyee and then some.

"Morris, this is a huge fish."

He seemed completely unmoved. He peered down at the salmon, then looked around us. The tide had carried us more than a mile past the hole where we had hooked the fish.

"Are we going to fish here?" was all Morris said.

"We have to head back up there." I pointed up the channel to a tiny cluster of boats in the distance.

"Why can't we just fish here?" asked Morris.

We had drifted into a small shallow bay that produced flounder and the occasional rock cod.

"But, Morris"—I tried to keep the exasperation from my voice; I really didn't want to be away from the action—"we know there's fish up there."

"Well, all right then, let's not sit around here all day."

Morris sounded impatient. He had just landed the biggest fish I had seen all summer, but apparently all he could think about was the time he had spent away from his speech.

I put the tyee into the fish box and cleaned the blood out of the boat, and we headed back to the Second Hole. A few people called out to Morris asking about his fish, but he just waved at them and went back to his papers.

The rest of our time in the back eddy was uneventful. Morris proceeded to mumble to himself as before, and I took up a position that would keep us out of the way of the rest of the guides. By the time we left to go to the lodge for dinner, I doubt Morris even remembered catching anything. He jumped out of the boat as soon as I had it tied to the dock. He walked off, clutching his speech. It was up to me to manhandle the salmon out of the fish box and haul it to the weigh scales.

There were a few people standing about the dock or sunning themselves on the yachts. As I staggered past them there was a collective gasp as they noticed what I was carrying.

"Oh my God," someone called out.

"Morris, did you catch that fish?"

"Oh, Morris, it's huge!"

Word of a fish this big spreads magically. People began appearing on the decks of the other yachts. They hurried down from the main lodge and the cabins. A crowd of admirers suddenly surrounded Morris. He stopped walking away and joined me at the scales. I dropped the slab of a fish on the hook and adjusted the balance beam. The fish weighed in at thirty-eight pounds: the biggest fish caught at the lodge so far that year. The excitement swelled; men were patting Morris on the back, offering him drinks, and someone handed him a cigar. A beautiful woman was stroking his arm affectionately. It began to sink in. Morris realized what he had accomplished. He began to answer the questions everybody had.

I took the fish off the scales and lugged it to the cleaning table. I hoisted the fish onto it, got out my cleaning knife, and then realized I hadn't asked Morris what he wanted to do with it. A tyee is often trophy mounted: frozen whole and taken to the taxidermist without being cleaned. I made my way back through the crowd of people around Morris. He was too busy recounting his adventures to notice me.

I came up beside him in time to hear him say, "Well, you know, my guide thought it was just a stick."

nine **THE EXPERT**

IT WASN'T FOR Morris but as a favour to Nelson that I was at the dock as the yacht pulled in the next day. I sat in the comfort of my boat and watched as the crew, dressed in crisp white uniforms, secured the mooring lines. I always enjoyed watching a practised and efficient crew going about their duties, but Morris spoiled the effect. He stood at the railing and fussed, yelling unnecessary and contradictory orders to a crew that obviously knew their business. They managed to get the mooring lines tied and the gangplank steps set out in spite of his help.

Morris and his guests were down the steps and onto the dock immediately, their faces filled with eagerness. They were ready to go fishing. This was not a good sign.

Serious fishermen, the kind I prefer to take fishing, are never in a rush. Fish have been in the water for thousands of years. They will always be hungry. There is always time for some calm reflection over a refreshment. A little planning time for what lies ahead. One shouldn't hurry these things. It doesn't do to charge off to the fishing holes and then discover you've overlooked something—not enough beer, perhaps, or too much gin and not enough vodka.

This much enthusiasm meant these people entertained some fantasy fishing adventure, no doubt thanks to Morris. They were completely divorced from the reality of the situation. The rest of the guides for the party hadn't arrived yet. It was up to me to be the good host. I got out of my boat and joined the little knot of people on the dock.

Morris introduced me to two of them, a couple in their mid-fifties. He presented them to me as though they were exotic birds, their plumage delicate and easily damaged.

"So, you're Dave," the man said, giving my hand a shake that would have crushed a walnut. "Morris has told us all about you."

I could only imagine. The man put his arm around my shoulder and gave me a conspiratorial wink, one fisherman to another.

"Now I want you to know that I'm a world-class fisherman. I've caught fish all over the world. Isn't that right, Morris? Marlin in the Caribbean, tarpon off the Florida Keys, sailfish on the west coast of Mexico—more fish and places than I care to mention, more than my share of salmon, too. It doesn't matter to me if I never catch another fish but," and here he paused for effect, "the little woman here has never done this before. It would mean a lot to me if you make sure she catches a couple of nice ones."

He paused again to give me a look that suggested great riches would be mine if I could make it happen.

"Do you think you could do that for me, Dave?" He gave me a little nudge with his fist.

I didn't know how to reply. I was in awe. This guy was world-class all right, but it had nothing to do with catching fish. The thought of spending the next four hours in a small boat with him left me truly speechless. I checked out the "little woman."

She stood to one side and slightly behind him. The sun shone out of a cloudless sky, and she was in the shadow of the man, both literally and figuratively. She stood there quietly and observed the scene. The events of the next few hours, however, would suggest she was just using him for shade.

"So, this is your boat," he said. His voice carried a tone of disappointment. "You like these metal boats better than fibreglass?"

The tone seemed to suggest a moral failure on my part. Here was a world-class angler, and I expected him to use questionable equipment?

Long ago I stopped explaining to people why I chose to do things the way I did. I got tired of hearing myself explain how a metal boat could be beached on the rocks without having any harm come to it. People that wouldn't dream of hovering over a plumber or a mechanic to offer advice can't seem to stop themselves when it comes to fishing; for some reason, they have to prove themselves. Of course they will always be at a disadvantage. The conditions and style of fishing at Stuart Island are unique. No matter how much fishing this guy had done, he could never understand the way we did things until he kept quiet and paid attention. A true fisherman would have known this.

"I would have thought you'd have a centre console on a boat like this. Isn't it awkward steering the boat from the stern like that?"

My boat is equipped with a large motor (Vop's fingerprints embedded in the paint) for running out to the fishing holes and a smaller one to fish with when I get there. Both of the motors have a tiller arm for steering and throttle control. The tiller arm gives quicker responses in the rapids than a steering wheel. The response is not only quicker but subtler. It gives you more of a "feel" for what the water is doing. I didn't bother to explain all this. I just redirected his attention, "Ummm . . . do you think you'll be warm enough?"

He was wearing a light windbreaker, a polo shirt, and a pair of Fortrel slacks. He was warm enough to be on the dock in the sunshine, but the conditions on the water are very different. The wind and the extremely cold temperature of the water combine to make even the hottest summer days very cool in the rapids. I noticed his wife was bundled up in a sweater and a Floater coat.

"Maybe we should grab another Floater coat. It can get pretty cold out on the—"

"I'll be fine."

He cut me off abruptly. I also got a look flashed in my direction that closed any further discussion of the subject. I was coming dangerously close to questioning his manhood. I helped them into the boat, untied the ropes, and we set off.

The tide was just turning to ebb. We headed north along the mainland and followed the wide sweep of Vancouver Bay.

At the north end of the bay the shoreline changes to rocky cliffs. It makes a sharp turn into a narrow passage between the mainland and Stuart Island. The passage continues to the north and eventually opens out into Bute Inlet. A huge volume of water must pass through it each day as the tides flow back and forth. This is the Arran Rapids. During a big tide the current runs at over fifteen knots. It has a reputation as one of the most dangerous stretches of water on the coast. On the ebb tide the water passes the cliffs on the way out of the inlet, forming a back eddy against them. You can tuck inside this shelter just a few feet away from the current raging past. This fishing hole is on the opposite shore from Stuart Island, so it's known as the Far Side.

The Far Side is only a mile and a half from the resort, no more than ten minutes away in my boat, but, in an open boat doing thirty-five knots, my world-class fisherman was already feeling the cold. His lips were turning blue by the time we arrived at the hole.

"Mm-m-m-man, look at that eagle! Isn't that a mm-m-m-magnificent bird." He pointed a shaky finger in the direction of a twisted fir tree that clung precariously to the cliff. The combination of the cold and his admiration for the bird gave his face a slightly demented appearance.

"Look at him up there. Isn't that wonderful. I can see why our forefathers chose them as our national symbol."

He seemed to imply these were my forefathers as well. Guys like this tended to forget such small matters as international borders and national sovereignty. I swear I could almost hear the American anthem swelling in the background.

The cliffs at the Far Side continue deep into the water where the bottom drops off steeply—a few feet from shore the water is already 200 or 300 feet deep. I handed out the rods, baited the hooks with herring, and told them to go down to 140 feet.

The man looked at me suspiciously. With his rod sticking straight out from the side of the boat, his rod tip was no more than 30 feet from the rocks.

"Are you sure you want me to go down that far? That's pretty deep, isn't it?"

His wife was already letting her line down the way I had shown her.

"If you want to get down to where the fish are, then 140 feet is where you want to be."

He gave me a sly smile, as though I might be setting him up for something. He cupped his hand over the reel to hide it from me as he let the line out. He stopped and clicked the brake on. I estimated he was down at the most 60 feet. His wife's line, going down the full 140 feet, took much longer. She had barely reached that level and flicked her brake on when her rod tip began to twitch up and down.

"Quick, reel up, fast as you can!" I yelled at her excitedly.

The husband looked at me as if I'd gone nuts, but his wife did as she was told. She kept reeling as fast as she could. The fish headed straight up toward the boat with the herring in its mouth—she had to catch up to it and set the hook before the salmon could spit out the bait. Her rod bent over into the water, and I had her jerk the rod to set the hook. An eight- or nine-pound salmon jumped clear of the water and dashed furiously about the surface.

I asked the husband to reel his line in to get out of the way, but he was too slack-jawed in surprise to be of much use. I took his rod out of his hands and reeled the line in myself. He only had 50 feet of line out, so it didn't take me too long.

The fish took a couple of short runs before allowing itself to be brought to the side of the boat where I could put it in the net. The wife jumped up and down with excitement; her husband was out of his seat, patting her on the back.

"Marvellous, marvellous, that's wonderful, dear, just wonderful."

I hit the fish on the head with a club to kill it and put it away in the fish box built into the stern of my boat, and we went back to fishing.

The tide was running a little stronger, small whirlpools forming at the edges of the eddy, and the main current running through the passage had an obvious flow to it. The current in the eddy pulled against the rods, bending them toward the water. I had to keep an eye on them to detect any movements that might tell of a salmon. The man was shivering so hard by now it was difficult to tell anything from the tip of his; the supple rod amplified the trembling in his hands.

The first strong surge of the tide caught the woman's attention.

"Oh my, oh my, look at that water! Just look at the way that water is moving." She turned to me and asked, "What do they call this again?"

The man spoke up before I could answer. "That's the Campbell River, dear. Say, Dave, and how far is the town itself?"

Before I could find a diplomatic way of explaining to the man that he didn't know what the hell he was talking about, the line began screaming off his wife's reel again. I got the husband to reel up this time, and then turned the boat and chased after the fish.

It was bigger than the first one and put up much more of a fight. I had to coach her, telling her what to do to land the fish.

Her husband stood beside her, repeating anything I said. It was as if I was speaking a foreign language and he had to translate for her.

I would say, "Now keep your rod tip up."

And he would say, "Keep your rod tip up, dear."

"That's it, now start reeling."

"Start reeling, honey."

"The fish wants to run, let him take some line."

"We want you to let the fish run, sweetheart."

"Okay, reel in the line again."

"Reel in now, dear."

"That's good, now lift the rod up so I can get the net over its head."

"It's time to net the fish, darling. Lift the rod up so we can get the net over its head."

The poor fish didn't stand much of a chance against the three of us. I managed to get the fish in the boat and shook the woman's hand. The man was patting her on the back again, but you could tell he wasn't as excited as with the first one. There wasn't much ceremony either, and we got back to fishing quickly.

I watched him again as he let his line down. This time he went to eighty feet. He seemed to be giving the situation some thought.

"Why do all you guides use such long rods? Wouldn't it be easier with a shorter rod? I mean, you saw the way my wife was shaking trying to control the fish at the boat. Wouldn't a shorter rod give you more control over the fish when you go to put it in the net? It doesn't make sense to me."

I didn't think it would be wise to point out that his wife was the only one who knew how well the rods worked so far.

"A sensitive rod like these," I tried to explain, "allows me to see whether a fish is biting or not."

"How can you tell that?"

"Well, by the way the tip of the rod moves."

"You can tell just by the way my rod moves if I've got a fish on?"

He was clearly skeptical.

"So, you're trying to tell me that from where you're sitting you can see the fish before I know it's there. Just by the way the rod moves?"

"Sure," I said, "it looks just like that."

I pointed at his wife's rod, which was bouncing up and down about a foot.

Once again he had to reel up. Once again I turned the boat and we followed the fish as it ran out into the tide. This salmon was even bigger than the last two, and it took twenty minutes of careful work to bring the fish to the side of the boat. The man remained in his seat this time. He looked glum.

His wife and I landed the fish. It was a beautiful eighteen-pound spring salmon. I hit it on the head. I put the fish in the fish box and cleaned some blood off the side of my boat.

When I turned back to my guests, the husband was rolling something around on the floor of the boat with his finger.

As soon as I saw what he had, I realized what must have happened.

When I'd hit the fish, the lens of one of its eyes had popped off and was lying on the floor. A lens clear and round, like a small marble. It was definitely one of these that he was rolling around on the deck.

I've learned over the years to sit back and simply observe. You never know when you might learn something, especially when you are dealing with an expert.

The man cleared his throat, "Gerry, do you see this?"

He sounded like the narrator of a Jacques Cousteau undersea special.

"This is what they call an immature salmon egg."

"Oh really," said his wife. "How can you tell it's immature?"

That was a good question. I wanted to know the answer to that one myself. Salmon eggs come in big clumps called skeins that contain fifteen hundred or so small eggs. They can be pink in colour, or anywhere from red to yellow, but I've never seen a clear one in all the years I've been cleaning salmon.

"Well, you see they are clear like this when they are very young."

"Oh my, you mean we just killed a mother?"

I couldn't stand it anymore. I started the big motor and took us back to the fishing hole. A strong current gets pushed out of Vancouver Bay to the north to collide with the Far Side back eddy. The two currents come together at the back end of the hole and a large whirlpool can form there. It's the spot where Wet Lenny earned his nickname.

When we pulled into the back eddy the tide was running hard. The front end nearest the cliffs was a churning mass of whitewater by now. The boats trying to fish there all crowded against the shore. Small, fast moving, and very dangerous whirlpools formed in the back eddy, and all the guides were scrambling to stay out of their way. With three fish in the boat already, I decided not to fight the back eddy and all the other boats huddled against the cliffs. I stopped just inside Vancouver Bay, short of the spot where the two currents came together. I had them drop their lines.

"Are we fishing here?" the husband asked.

I resisted the temptation to make a smart remark.

"Yes, that's right," I replied blandly.

"Why don't we fish where we were?"

"There'll be fish here as well," I said, trying to reassure him. "Besides, we don't want to fight with all those boats up there."

"Well, shouldn't we be closer to the cliffs?"

He pointed to the spot where Wet Lenny's whirlpool formed.

"A whirlpool lives there," I said, nodding my head in the direction he was pointing. He turned and looked closely at the water as if waiting for one to appear on cue. A thin line of driftwood and floating kelp was the only indication of the tideline. He gave me another one of his sly grins. He obviously thought that now I had some fish in the boat, I was trying to slack off.

"I don't see anything like that. Why don't we just try it there and see what happens? This doesn't look like a good spot at all."

"I know what happens there," I said affably. "We get eaten by a whirlpool."

"You don't really think we're going to catch anything here do you?"

Once again, before I had time to reply, his wife interrupted us. She had been sitting there quietly, patiently watching the tip of her rod the way I had asked her.

"Ummm ... David, something is pulling on my line."

Her rod bent over in half and the line disappeared under the boat. I turned the boat and spun out of the way of the line. The husband grudgingly reeled in his line. She was getting quite good at playing a salmon. It only took a short time before we had another one in the boat.

With four springs on board we had reached our bag limit for the day. It was time to head back to the dock.

By now the warm afternoon sun was low on the mountains. As we ran back the husband was hunched over, shivering and looking miserable: Napoleon on his retreat from Moscow. His wife looked warm and toasty, nestled into her heavy sweater and Floater coat.

He didn't move when we reached the dock. He sat staring at his feet while I tied up the boat.

Gerry reached over and patted him on the knee. It was the playful gesture of a woman half her age. "Look at it this way, dear"—she smiled, a slight, enigmatic smile that reminded me of a certain painting I had seen—"at least it's teaching you humility."

He sat bolt upright. "Humility," he sputtered, "humility!" His nostrils flared and he glared at the two of us. "Why, I haven't got any humility." He stood up, stepped out of the boat, and stalked off down the dock.

I must have sat there with my mouth open. Gerry patted me on the knee with that same gesture again. She was enjoying herself. She was almost flirting.

"Don't worry about him, dear. He gets the same way when I beat him at tennis."

ten **THE FELLOWSHIP OF THE SEA**

IT HAD TAKEN much time and effort, but the four men had planned the perfect long weekend of fishing. They had known one another for years. They had gone to the same high school and been members of the same fraternity at university. They were able to trust one another in ways they could trust no one else. One of them had offered the use of his yacht. They explained to their wives how they planned to take the boat out of Lake Washington, through the locks, and cruise up to Stuart Island. The yacht would be moored at Herbert Crane's resort for the summer, and if they left Thursday morning and ran all night, they could be at the island by Friday afternoon with plenty of time for fishing. They would then fly back to Seattle on a regular float plane run.

It was going to be a guys' weekend, they explained to the wives. The wives knew what that meant: no shaving, old fishing sweaters, fish blood and herring scales everywhere. Of course, the women didn't want to come this time. Instead they packed the yacht's freezer full of food and made sure their husbands had clean socks and a change of underwear.

The men knocked off work early on Wednesday; they were self-employed or owned their own companies, so they could do as they liked. The boat was fuelled and ready to go. The wives kissed them goodbye. The men eased the yacht away from the dock and headed out into the crisp morning air. They set a course for the locks. The fresh air in their faces made them all feel alive.

The women decided it would be a laugh to surprise their husbands at the locks when the boat went through. They could have a pleasant morning drive, wave to their husbands as they passed by, and then have lunch somewhere nice, maybe even do some shopping on the way back. They all piled in the car and headed for the freeway.

The men, meanwhile, made a little stop along the way. It was going to be a long weekend, and they needed some extra supplies.

The women knew from experience how long it took to get to the locks and timed their arrival accordingly. Their husbands' boat was nowhere in sight, so they relaxed and watched the other yachts passing by. They waved to the people on board. One of the women remarked on the camaraderie around boats; you didn't find it anywhere else. Strangers would always wave at one another and smile. People never did that elsewhere—could you imagine waving at people as they drove past in their cars, for instance? You certainly wouldn't think of doing it to people as you passed them in the street. They would think you were mad! Yet, somehow, when you were on a boat all this changed.

The people on the passing yachts waved back at the women who happily waited for their husbands. The wives soon saw the boat in the distance. As it came closer they jumped up and down, waving.

Four bikini-clad women, sunning themselves in the shelter of the flying bridge, noticed the ladies waving along the shore.

"Oh look!" said one of them. "It's so fun how friendly people are when you're on a boat!"

The four women on the boat all stood up and waved to the nice ladies on the shore.

eleven **THE FOOL**

WITH THE BOATS in the water and working properly, the house organized, and the first few days of guiding done, Vop and I slipped back into our routine. A kind of timelessness settled over us, a sense that the winter had never happened. We had never started or stopped. There was no beginning or end. We had always guided and we always would guide, endlessly.

There are people who say the time you spend fishing is not deducted from your lifespan. If this is true, the guides here have pushed that notion to its farthest limits; time exerts the same pull on us that gravity exerts on a feather. Vop and I floated in a region outside time.

We were playing a game of dominoes. As if to give reality to the winter that had just passed, Vop told me about the woman he had met while at university.

I had met some of Vop's previous girlfriends. They were from the surrounding islands and had all grown up in the rainforest. They had names like Fern or Apple, Sparkle and Aura. They would appear and disappear like wraiths, paddling in to the beach below the house in kayaks or canoes. They used kayaks the way people in the city might use a bicycle. They were without guile or artifice, wore no makeup, and were completely at ease with their bodies. They were as comfortable with nudity as they were in the loose skirts and sweaters they wore. These women had no tan lines.

Vop had spent the winter attending classes at a small university in Nelson, BC. We had talked about his decision the previous summer. The larger institutions in Vancouver had accepted him, but Vop had chosen the small town so he wouldn't be distracted. For Vop, a trip into Campbell River was considered going to the city. Not that he was naive in the ways of the world. He just felt he would get more work done in a less hectic environment.

While he was there, he met Carol. She was a couple of years older and a year ahead of him at the school. For Vop this gave her an air of worldliness and sophistication that left him feeling intimidated and tongue-tied in her presence. She wore perfume.

Carol had grown up in Nelson, where the school was located. Her grandparents were Doukhobors who had emigrated from Russia and settled in the Slocan Valley. Her parents had drifted away from the orthodox views and raised their daughter as a Canadian. She had gone to movies and hockey games, eaten in restaurants, and gone skiing in the winter. On the ski hills she had met people from all over the world. She still retained something of her grandparents' tradition. She was a sensible girl suspicious of flash and careful when it came to taking chances. She wasn't a prude, but she had little patience with foolish people. Her friends teased her about being too serious.

Carol had taken a job on the ski hills to earn money to go to school. Family vacations were spent on the lakes and mountains not far from home. She had never seen the Pacific Ocean. She had never met anyone like Vop either. He was totally unlike any of the men she usually associated with. He was more like the visiting wild men of the ski slopes, the ones always getting in trouble by skiing out of bounds or racing down impossible cliff faces, out of control. As she got to know him she found he had a more serious side. He had a knowledge of gardening and the use of wild plants and mushrooms that would have impressed even her grandparents. She found herself intrigued and frightened by him at the same time. It was an irresistible combination. Vop entertained her with stories of the coast, and in his laid-back way they became friends. Vop soon realized he wanted more than that.

They both had a full schedule of classes and homework, which left little time for a courtship. Even if the time could be found, neither of them had money to spend on entertainment or eating out.

Vop was frustrated. He wanted to take things further but didn't know how to do it. He had never faced a situation like this with the girls he had known. This made Carol all the more desirable. Vop needed some dramatic gesture to find a way to her heart.

One day Carol was joking about her financial situation. All her money was going to tuition, rent, and food, so she was cutting costs where she could; she had resorted to an old standby in her bathroom. Vop was shocked that such a beautiful and sophisticated lady was forced to use the Canadian Tire catalogue in such a fashion.

He saw an opportunity.

He was living in residence in the university dormitories. The bathrooms at the end of the hall had an endless supply of bathroom tissue. Vop went around and collected an armload. He found the prospect of visiting her at home a bit daunting, so he fortified himself with several beers.

By the time Vop was ready to leave, a light rain was beginning to fall and the sun was on the way down. Hunched protectively over his armload of vulnerable paper, he walked off into the gathering twilight.

Carol lived in a small cottage, once the caretaker's shack for a now closed gravel pit. The university and its residences were situated above it on the side of a low mountain. A road went from the college down the hill, to the edge of the gravel pit. There it turned to one side of it and joined up with the main road into town.

Vop was concerned about the paper getting wet if he took the long way. There was a soft mound of sandy clay mixed with gravel that sloped from the campus nearly to Carol's doorstep and the mouth of the gravel pit, both 150 feet below. He knew about the pit: the rim dropped straight off for eight feet or so. Vop felt confident. He had negotiated hillsides like this before with no problems. The low fence separating the road from the edge of the pit was no obstacle, even with his arms full. He strolled over to the edge and stepped off into space.

Carol was enjoying a quiet night at home. She shared the house with a couple of other students who were all out for the night. She was catching up on some schoolwork. Her desk lamp was the only light on. The sound of classical music settled around her like a shawl. The wind had picked up and was driving the rain against the windows. She heard a scratching sound outside but paid no attention; there were many low branches on the nearby trees that could scrape against the sides of the house.

But the faint noise persisted.

It sounded like it was coming from the direction of the front door. Still she dismissed it as the scraping of a branch. Then came a definite knock. She put down her book and got up to investigate. She opened the front door carefully.

A horrible pink and grey apparition lurched at her out of the shadows, shuffling into the light cast by the bare bulb on the porch. Carol backed up instinctively. Chunks of gravel and clay clung to the tattered rags it wore. It seemed to be oozing blood from several places. The thing thrust out an arm toward her. The hand was holding what appeared to be a soggy, mud-stained half-roll of toilet paper. A pitiful mumble issued from the clay-encrusted hole of a mouth.

"Here, Carol, I brought you a present."

Carol was a kind and charitable soul. She helped the soaked, muddy, and bleeding Vop into the house and ran him a hot bath. Afterwards she bandaged his wounds and put him to bed on the couch.

"The next day," said Vop, finishing the story, "we looked outside. You could see where I hit, lost my balance with all that toilet paper in my arms, and then rolled down the hill. That slope wasn't as gentle, or the gravel as soft, as it looked from the edge. The toilet paper followed me down, unrolling as it went. It lay there like so many party streamers down the face of the gravel pit. The damn stuff stayed like that until a snowfall covered it up a few weeks later.

"If you don't believe me, you can ask Carol about it. She's coming to work here this summer."

I knew Vop well enough by now not to question most of his stories. Besides, who would want to make up something like that?

I was curious to meet the fair Carol. After hearing Vop's stories all winter and never having seen the Pacific Ocean, Carol had applied for a job at the Carringtons' resort just next door to us. With her experience at the ski hills, getting hired was no problem.

twelve **THE FRUIT DOESN'T
FALL FAR FROM THE TREE**

GARY WAS GETTING impatient with his father. He had been
tinkering with the outboards for over an hour now and still
couldn't get them to work. He was being very stubborn about
asking Nelson for help. Herbert had brought the boat and
motors brand new in Campbell River the week before. Nelson
had flown to town with them and driven the boat back. It was
a twenty-foot Boston whaler, top of the line, the best one they
had on hand at the dealership. It had a centre console, in shining chrome; highly polished wood trim; and an impressive array
of antennae, aerials, and flagpoles with flags and pennants that
flapped in the wind. The whaler had a huge outboard to run out
to the fishing holes, which looked like a refrigerator clamped
onto the back of the boat. Beside it was a smaller motor, used for
fishing. At the moment neither one of them would start.

For the first week Herbert was seen everywhere. With
the sun flashing off the new chrome and the flags, aerials, and
antennae all erect, a company of mounted knights in full heral-
dic display could not have presented a more imposing sight.
For that first week the boat had performed beautifully. It was a
thing of wonder as it sliced effortlessly through the water from
one fishing hole to the next.

Herbert and Gary waved to all the guides and yelled to
them across the back eddies. They felt like a part of the scene.
Their enthusiasm was dampened only a little by the fact that
they hadn't caught any salmon so far. Now, however, both

motors refused to start, and the sleek whaler remained tied to the dock. Herbert squatted in the stern of the boat and fiddled.

Gary wandered off down the dock and stood at the end of the finger float. He watched an eagle in a tree. It was in a tall snag across from the resort, on the other side of Canoe Pass. The pass was barely wide enough for a guide boat to navigate and separated Mermaid Island from the mainland. Canoeists and kayakers used it to bypass the dangerous Dent Rapids. On big tides the water roared through, white and foaming. The guides would thread their way through it, dodging the rocks inches below the surface, throwing up sheets of spray. Gary fantasized about running it in the whaler one day, but for now he was content to watch the tide swirl past and the eagles hunched in the trees.

Two tiny specks rounded the point of Mermaid Island and headed for the pass. Gary could make out the rhythmic flash of the kayak paddles as they reflected the sun. They grew steadily larger, the efficient paddle strokes closing the distance with remarkable speed. Gary was so absorbed watching the paddlers that he didn't notice me as I pulled into the dock ahead of them. As I tied the boat up they passed by the spot where he was standing. I heard him call over to them.

"Hey, where are you going?"

The kayaks looked well equipped for a long journey. They were obviously not just out for the day.

"Juneau," one of the kayakers yelled back at him.

Gary looked puzzled.

"How am I supposed to know," he yelled back indignantly, "I'm the one that's asking you."

thirteen  **YULE TIDE**

I STOPPED BY Nelson's place to check the mail and do some business. I also knew things were quiet enough for a short visit. I wanted to catch up on the events of the previous winter at Stuart Island. It was more than just idle curiosity. There were thirty-five or forty hardy souls that spent the winters at the island. Some were caretakers, others were the owners and managers that ran the resorts, as well as their families. It was a small social circle. The isolation threw people together in ways that created strong bonds, both of friendship and intense hatred. It helped me, as an independent guide working for all of them, to find out who was still talking to whom. I needed to know who got drunk at the Christmas party and made a pass at someone else's wife. Some feuds still simmered after years. If I was to keep peace between myself and the people I was to work for this summer, it was important not to mention the wrong person at the wrong moment.

As I passed I said hello to Herbert as he poked about inside his brand new outboard. He looked like someone staring into a refrigerator and trying to decide lunch. He could only grunt in reply.

Nelson was making a fresh pot of coffee when I entered the lodge kitchen. We sat down at the kitchen table with a steaming mug apiece. We chatted idly about the winters' events and the latest convolutions in local politics. Nelson kept to himself as much as possible. He tried not to take one side or the other. However, this winter he had taken on a higher profile in the community, or at least a wider one. He had played Santa Claus at the Christmas party.

"So what's this I hear about you almost buying it in the rapids after the party?" I asked him.

"Oh yeah, that was way too close. Who told you about it?"

"Troutbreath."

"Old Troutbreath does have a tendency to exaggerate. I'd better tell you how it really happened."

Nelson had the resort all to himself over Christmas. His wife had gone to visit relatives while he stayed behind to look after the property; it was the perfect opportunity to fulfill one of his dreams and play Santa Claus for the kids. The Community Association rented the costume and on the night of the party, suitably padded and dressed, he used his guide boat as a sleigh to deliver the presents. His Santa was a big hit. He was much more effusive than the dryly reserved Mr. Carrington, the Santa of the previous three years. The kids loved Nelson and, after they had gone to bed, the adults made sure he was rewarded with plenty of the Christmas spirit. The party went late into the night. It was past two in the morning when Santa swayed down the last dock and left for home.

It was a pitch-black night, and on the water Nelson could hardly see his hand in front of his face. He had made the trip at night dozens of times; he could find his way by the outlines of the mountains and the position of the stars. Once he got through the rapids and past the small group of islands in mid-channel, he would be able to see the lights he had left on at the resort. He had timed his trip home near slack tide so that he wouldn't need to worry about whirlpools. When he left Big Bay the tide was still flowing slowly on the flood. Nelson kept his eyes on the dim shapes of the mountains so he wouldn't get pushed off course. He was close to the mid-channel islands when it happened.

Someone was towing a house through the rapids on a log raft. There were no lights on the towboat or on the house itself. In the pitch-black, Nelson had no chance to see it. His boat hit the raft a glancing blow and pitched over onto its side, flipping Nelson into the freezing water. The towboat and house kept on going. The people on board probably didn't even know a boat had hit them. Nelson, suddenly sober, found himself alone in the rapids, treading water in a Santa suit.

The absurdity of the situation was not lost on him. It was absurd, yet very desperate. There was no one at the resort to come looking for him if he didn't arrive on time. No one at the party could know what had happened. It was the middle of winter. There was no hope of rescue.

He tried to relax and think clearly about what he could do to help himself. The tide was turning to the ebb. Perhaps the current would carry him to one of the small islands nearby. He bobbed along, trying to conserve energy. The Santa suit was bulky enough to help keep him afloat and it warmed him slightly. He felt he could last until he reached the shore.

However, it soon became apparent that he'd drifted past the nearest land. Cruelly, he could make out the lights of his resort. He might just as well try swimming toward the stars above him. He struck out swimming anyway; it was better than drifting helplessly. If he was going to drown he was not going to give in without a struggle. He started giggling, it was so ridiculous, and he didn't want to drown dressed as Santa Claus. What would the people that came looking for his body think? Would they see the humour in the situation? He doubted it.

He kept on swimming. He hoped to catch the back eddy behind the islands—maybe that would drift him back to them again. He didn't know now how he'd kept it up. His arms were getting tired lifting the sleeves of the sodden suit, but he didn't want to take it off, it was warmer than nothing at all. The water was so cold he should already have passed out from hypothermia. He struggled on, but his arms ached. It would be so much easier to just drift and close his eyes.

Then his hand touched something.

His hand was numb from the cold and at first he thought it was a log, a piece of driftwood. If he could cling to it he could use it for a raft. He reached out with both hands. It was smooth and rose steeply above his head. The cold dulled his brain. It took him some time to realize what it was. He couldn't believe his good fortune. It was his boat! He and his boat had drifted together. The reunion gave him a new rush of energy—all he needed to pull himself out of the water and into the boat. He was suddenly back in the seat he had left so abruptly.

Everything was still intact—the boat must have righted itself after he was thrown out. The motor had stalled and the boat had drifted with the tide.

Nelson started the outboard and went home.

He walked me down to the dock as I was leaving. He had noticed Herbert with his head in the outboards, and he was curious.

"I'd better go down there and check on him."

Herbert rose and wiped his hands on a rag as we approached.

"Having a little engine trouble?"

Nelson tried to sound casual.

"Ummm . . . yeah, I can't get either one of them to start. They were working perfectly the other day. I don't understand it."

Nelson stepped into the boat and tried the electric start on the big engine. The starter motor clicked into life and whined in protest. Nelson turned it off before he did any damage to it. He grabbed the starter cord on the small engine and tried to give it a pull. It wouldn't budge. The cowling on the engine was off and he gave the flywheel a turn with both hands. It wouldn't turn.

"Herbert, these engines are seized tight."

"What do you mean?"

Herbert clearly had a slim grasp of outboard mechanics. Nelson tried to explain it to him as simply as possible.

"They're stuck. The pistons won't move in the cylinders. Herbert, your power head has fused into one piece of metal."

"Is that bad?"

"Well, it couldn't be much worse."

"I don't know how it could have happened."

Nelson had to phrase the next question carefully.

"Herbert, you remember the conversation we had about two-cycle engines, about how you have to put oil in the gas?"

"Come on now, you must think I'm a complete idiot. Of course I've been putting oil in the gas."

Herbert looked hurt.

"It's okay, Herbert, I just had to ask. I just can't think of anything else that would cause this to happen. Doesn't seem to be anything blocking the water pump."

Nelson regarded the two brand new but totally useless engines. He poked at the cowling lying on the floor with his toe. The signs were unmistakable; the engines were definitely fried. If it wasn't the oil, it could only be the water pump, but that was unlikely on such new engines. It was a puzzle—then something occurred to him. He finally cleared his throat, "Uh, Herbert, exactly where have you been getting the oil from?"

We both gave Herbert our expectant attention. Herbert thought it over carefully, then brightened and said, "I've been getting it from that forty-five-gallon drum of oil up by the generator shed."

Nelson shook his head in disbelief.

"Herbert, that stuff's for the crankcase of the generator. It's the same stuff you put in your car. You need a special two-stroke oil to mix with the gasoline. That oil won't blend with gas. It sits on the bottom of the gas tank and never gets to the engine. You've been running on straight gasoline all this time. I'm surprised the engines lasted as long as they did."

"Well," said Herbert, "I made sure I shook the gas tank the way you told me."

WORKERS ON GOVERNMENT SERVICE

fourteen

I WAS HOME cleaning out my boat after a particularly messy morning catching fish. I was taking a break from scrubbing, leaning on the long-handled brush like a highway worker filling a pothole, when I saw the RCMP boat passing the mouth of Big Bay. It was on its way up north again.

We used to see them stop in on a regular basis before they got their new boat. The government had replaced the aging cruiser they'd used for years with a new, advanced nautical system. The sleek and throbbing computerized craft was more spaceship than boat. They had given me a tour of it on one of their infrequent visits to the island. It was made of a special lightweight aluminum alloy. It had a revolutionary catamaran hull. The pontoons were capable of maintaining full speed in all but the most severe conditions, cleaving through the water like twin knives and giving a smooth and stable ride.

The wheelhouse had all the latest computerized navigational equipment. The pilot could track the exact location of the boat so precisely one could almost see it bobbing up and down on the display monitor. It received constant weather information, and a weather map was fed into the main computer display showing the conditions for five hundred miles around. There was a chart system on a CD-ROM that, as it was integrated into the radar, was capable of tracking the boat as it moved through the water. It showed the changing shoreline and all the navigational lights, channel markers, and marine hazards. They could travel at full speed even in fog or on the darkest night.

They couldn't tell me the top speed of the vessel. That was classified information, available only to those with the proper clearance.

That's where the problem began. While the top marine architects had designed the boat and the best minds in electronic engineering the electronics, the less glamorous day-to-day operations had been left to government bureaucracy. While everyone wanted to be associated with the high-tech sheen of the program, the task of managing the mundane service and supply had been considered beneath most people's job description. Somewhere in the maze that was the government department responsible, an assistant to the junior deputy minister had been given the task of supplying the crew with the food, water, and diesel needed to run the boat every day. This assistant didn't have the necessary clearance to know the top speed of the boat or its rate of fuel consumption. Not wanting to appear inept by asking his superiors (always the kiss of death in a bureaucracy), the assistant made up his own mind about the boat's requirements, deciding that such an impressive machine would have an equally impressive rate of fuel consumption. He certainly didn't want to experience the embarrassment of having the boat run out of gas—that wouldn't do much for his prospects for promotion, after all. He didn't know much about boats, but he knew how to order fuel, so he did. He ordered fuel suppliers up and down the coast to get ready by ordering a nearly endless supply.

The thing about the new boat was that the hull was unbelievably efficient. Its turbocharged twin diesels barely sipped out of the tanks, even at full power. When the crew realized how much fuel they had been assigned, they realized a mistake had been made. They notified the appropriate superior and were told to fill out a 24B/18-A in triplicate. The completed forms were to be submitted to the office in charge of service and supply, where the notice must proceed through the proper channels.

In the meantime they had to use up the fuel. They knew if they didn't there would be even more paperwork and their ability to obtain fuel in the future might be harmed. They began running the boat day and night, and at full speed whenever possible.

They would run the boat to the Alaska border, visit a remote First Nation reserve for a few hours, and then turn around and run all the way back to Vancouver. There they might ferry some VIP across the harbour for an hour and be off again.

I watched the boat flying past Big Bay and marvelled at the modern design. It cut through the waves with ease and efficiency. They always knew exactly where they were and where they were going, but, like a plague ship, they could never stop anywhere. They just kept driving on, flags waving gloriously in the wind, doing their duty by consuming the fuel the government, in its wisdom, had so generously given them.

fifteen TROUTBREATH

TROUTBREATH WAS THE dock boy for the Carringtons' marina. He was in charge of the moorage, organizing the guiding, selling bait, and running the gas pumps. He did his clothes shopping at the same place Nelson did, where he had found several overalls donated by an oil company. He was wearing one with TOM in a big red circle over the right breast pocket. He had three more of these outfits. One said BRAD, another BILL, and the last one announced, in gold letters, that he was a QUALIFIED TECHNICIAN. Troutbreath found that, by changing his appearance slightly and wearing a different overall, he could become four different people.

This appealed to his sense of chaos and his liking for uncertainty. Tourists would walk up to him and say, "Hey, I was talking to Bill yesterday. He was going to find something out for me. Have you seen him around?"

Troutbreath would point in the direction of the boathouse and say, "Yeah, I think I saw him going over that way earlier."

The people that worked in the boatshed would be equally as helpful: "Bill? Oh no, you just missed him. I think he was going over to the store."

The resort was quite a large complex; tourists could be kept on the hunt for a remarkably long time. You had to admire their persistence.

As a qualified technician, Troutbreath had done some work on a guy's motor, a high-performance outboard. The next day the guy returned for some minor adjustments. When Brad offered to do it for him the guy was quite adamant. "Oh no, I only want that qualified technician touching this baby."

Troutbreath watched the RCMP boat disappear behind the islands in mid-channel and then turned his attention to the tourist trying to dock his yacht at the gas float. The man was awkward with the controls, and the generic look of the yacht suggested that the boat was a rented one, probably out of Seattle. Yachts like this could be rented on the strength of a valid driver's licence and a current credit card. After much yelling back and forth between the man on the flying bridge and a woman, presumably the man's wife, standing on the deck ready to throw the ropes, the boat was secured.

The man climbed down from the flying bridge and approached Troutbreath with a worried look on his face. He cleared his throat and in a low voice said, "Say, uhhh... Tom... I was wondering if you could help me with a small problem."

Troutbreath had helped with small problems before.

"What seems to be the matter?" he asked.

"Keep your voice down please! I don't want my wife to hear us talking. She worries, you know."

Troutbreath adopted a more conspiratorial volume.

"Why don't you tell me what's wrong."

"It is kind of worrisome," the man said. "The bottom of the boat keeps filling up with water."

"I don't quite understand what you mean. The bottom of your boat?"

"You know, inside the boat, down where the engine is."

Troutbreath was slightly incredulous.

"You mean as we stand here talking your boat is filling with water?"

"Well, yes, it seems to do that every time we stop somewhere."

"Have you turned on the bilge pump?"

"The what pump?"

"You know, the bilge pump. It sucks up any water that gets in the boat."

"Uhhhh," said the man, looking a bit lost, "what's the bilge?"

Troutbreath looked at the man and then at the fifty-five-foot yacht he had piloted to the gas dock. He took the man on board and up to the wheelhouse. He pointed out the large switch labelled BILGE PUMP on the control panel. Troutbreath flipped on the switch. There was the sound of the pumps working, and then two heavy streams of water began pouring from the outlets in the hull.

"So that's a bilge pump."

The man was clearly impressed with Tom's expertise.

"Perhaps we should go down below and have a look. To see what's going on," Troutbreath suggested. He tried to remain as calm as possible. From the volume of water the pumps were moving it was clear that the boat was in danger of sinking.

Troutbreath and the man went below, into the engine room, where a set of floorboards gave access to the bilge. The boards were nearly floating. But the pumps kept up with the flow and the water began draining. There were no signs of a hole in the hull or other damage. Troutbreath was puzzled. The pumps continued to move water; it must be coming in from somewhere. He asked a few questions.

The yacht was indeed rented. It had been stored on dry land and dropped into the water on the day the man had picked it up. He and his wife had spent the next three days working their way up the coast. Every time they stopped somewhere the boat began filling with water. The water seemed to disappear as soon as they started running. This left the man in a difficult position. He didn't want to alarm his wife by telling her that the boat was sinking, but he was quickly using up all his excuses as to why they had to keep moving from one place to another. They had been running almost non-stop until they encountered the rapids.

"You haven't stopped running for two days?"

"I am starting to get a little tired."

"I don't suppose you've ever heard of a thing called a seacock?"

"Does it have something to do with the water?"

Troutbreath explained it for the man.

"A seacock is installed in the stern of the boat. When the boat is stored on dry land it allows any rainwater to drain out of the boat. This place in Seattle forgot to check it for you when they dropped the boat in the water."

He showed the man the compartment in the stern of the boat with the seacocks set into the bottom of it.

"See here," said Troutbreath, "when the boat is running, the water can drain out of these valves, but as soon as you stop, the water just flows in through them."

"Say, that is good to know. That sure makes me feel better."

"I've closed them now, so you won't have to worry about any more water getting in."

The two of them walked back to the bridge and the man offered Troutbreath a drink.

"I can't thank you enough. Is there any way I can repay you?"

"There's no need, that's what I'm here for. Is there anything else I can do for you?"

"Uh ... there is one more thing you can tell me."

"What's that?" asked Troutbreath.

The man pointed to the channel and the tide flowing past the mouth of the bay.

"Why does this river run both ways?"

sixteen **NEATNESS IS NOBILITY**

VOP AND I were sitting in our living room tying leaders. The dogfish had taken over the fishing holes and, as sharks will, were munching through anything that came in the way of their mouths, simply biting off our hooks along with the herring we used for bait. We needed to tie three or four dozen leaders a day just to keep up with the rate of attrition. Like people who knit, we were constantly surrounded by paraphernalia: spools of line, boxes of hooks, and small envelopes for coiling the finished leaders into.

A leader consists of two hooks and about four feet of line, the hooks artfully wrapped onto the line in a fashion proven to stand up to the stress of fighting a fish. Of course, each guide had their own method and considered all others suspect, even a sign of shoddy workmanship. Great care had to be taken so the line wrapped without kinking, looping over itself, or leaving flattened spots, or else the leader would break off on a fish.

Like knitting, after years of practice, it became an unconscious act. Vop and I gossiped as we tied. The university required Vop to live in the dormitories unless he could satisfy certain exemptions. Carol, for example, could prove she had resided in the township for the last twelve months. Vop had arrived in the final days before classes began. Most of the dorm rooms were already occupied. Vop found himself sharing a space with someone who wouldn't have been his first choice.

The room Vop was expected to live in left him sputtering with indignation. The dormitory was a cement block building, a filing cabinet for people. The rooms were about the size and shape of a shoebox. They were all identical. Each room was organized the same way on two sides: at the entrance was a door-less closet, then a set of double bunks, a series of shelves, and built-in desks for two people. These rooms had originally been designed to house four people back in the days when the college was a religious institution. Vop supposed people studying the Bible needn't worry about such worldly things as comfort and privacy. At the far end of the room was a large picture window with a fine view of the parking lot.

Vop's roommate in this space was about five years older, but the age gap could have been fifty years for all he and Vop had in common. He was a Greek man who had just spent the last four years in the Greek army. He was now studying engineering and had applied for the excellent school of engineering at UBC. However, that university did not accept first-year students from outside the country, so he was fulfilling this requirement at the much smaller college. He was not happy. He was not happy about the inferior school. He was not happy about the food in the cafeteria. He was certainly not happy about the constant rain and grey skies. He was very, very unhappy about his new roommate.

Vop agreed with his roommate's dissatisfaction on some points. Vop found the food in the cafeteria rather frightening as well. He was served some liver one night that was so tough he took it back to his room and fashioned a pair of sandals using the liver for the soles. He wore them back to the cafeteria the next day at dinner to prove his point. The sandals proved to be so comfortable and wore so well that he kept them for guiding. There were many areas, however, where Vop and his roommate would never be reconciled.

The Greek army had trained him well. In the closet, three suits were arranged with military precision, each suit an equal distance from the others like soldiers on a parade ground. Beneath the blue suit was a pair of brown shoes, perfectly aligned. The dark grey and the black pinstripe suits had black shoes neatly arranged the same way below them. The shoes were so highly polished Vop could see his face in them. Vop's roommate woke up precisely at 6:00 in the morning every day, whether he had classes or not. He stripped the blankets and top sheet off the bed, folded them, and placed them carefully under the pillow. The bottom sheet was tucked in so tightly you could bounce a quarter off it (Vop had tried this for himself). The roommate's books were arranged alphabetically on the shelves. The mathematics book had a small label on the edge of the shelf underneath it. The label read MATHEMATICS. Beneath the physics book was a label that read PHYSICS, and so on. The pencil on the desk was laid precisely beside the ruler, and the ruler was aligned neatly with the pen. A sign was taped to the wall by the desk that detailed man's hierarchy of needs. They formed a neat pyramid; at the top was the word SUCCESS. Vop couldn't find sex mentioned anywhere.

Vop had better things to do with his time than line up all his shoes with the laces tied. It's not that he was a slob or even inconsiderate, but he had different ideas about the things he wanted around him, like the liver sandals. He liked to go for long walks in the woods surrounding the campus. He was always bringing home things he found there, the big pine cones or interesting rocks. One day he found a deer skull complete with the antlers. He found a special spot for that on his desk.

Vop enjoyed the nightlife in town and visiting with new friends he made, dropping in on them unexpectedly sometimes. Quite often he wouldn't be out of bed until it was time for classes to start, so he had no time to make his bed. Vop made friends easily and they were always welcome to drop by. If they tracked a little mud into the place, Vop wasn't going to make them feel uncomfortable by pointing it out. That wasn't his idea of being a good host. As for laundry, well, with so much going on who could be expected to do it every day?

One evening when Vop came back to his room, he noticed there was a new sign taped above the windows. It stretched almost the full length of the wall and in large letters it read:

NEATNESS IS NOBILITY.

Vop regarded the sign carefully. It was clearly there as some sort of comment. And it was one that he wasn't about to let stand without making some sort of reply. He noticed the way the sign was arranged across the wall and an idea occurred to him.

He sat down and cut out a square of white paper and taped this over a strategic part of the sign, altering the gist of it completely. Vop stepped back and admired his handiwork. The room now had two signs on either side of it:

NEATNESS

on one side, and on Vop's,

NOBILITY.

seventeen WET LENNY

THE DOGFISH WERE partly responsible for Wet Lenny earning his nickname. He usually didn't fish the rapids much. They lacked a certain precision that his style of fishing needed. He certainly didn't spend much time in the chaos that was the Far Side, but if powerboats couldn't stay in the back eddy, neither could the dogfish. The water there flushed the dogfish out; they're lazy swimmers and didn't want to fight the rapids. When they show up in the area in great numbers, the rapids become the only refuge. At such times grown men have been reduced to tears by the futility of trying to keep a herring in the water.

Lenny had fallen out of his boat before. Once he was trying to net a fish that was just out of reach. His feet slipped out from under him and he pitched forward, head first, into the water. This happened to people on occasion but, as Wet Lenny had lost the fish by falling in, it was considered unprofessional.

Then there was the time he was attempting to remove some line tangled around his propeller (another reason he didn't venture into the rapids). Lenny tilted up the outboard but neglected to lock it into position. He leaned out over the stern, clinging to the motor, and reached out to the prop. It looked like he was riding the outboard; his arms were wrapped around it like those of a man clinging to the neck of a horse. The motor must have decided it didn't want to be ridden. It tipped back down into the water with Lenny still riding it. That was a little stupid perhaps, but still not enough to earn a nickname.

The fateful day on which Lenny became Wet Lenny started quietly enough. Spring was turning into summer and the big tides were waning. The water slipped past the back eddy like drifting smoke. It gurgled like a well-fed baby. The sun was now hot on the skin, and some guests were fishing with their shirts off. Others fell asleep with their heads on their chests. Even the guides were showing signs of drowsiness. They struggled to stay awake behind dark glasses. You could almost forget the danger.

The whirlpool at the back of the Far Side watched and waited.

One of Lenny's lines had been bitten off by a dogfish and tangled with itself—what was left of the leader line was wrapped up around the weight, and he had to re-tie the whole set-up. Lenny hunched over, concentrating on his knots. Each one had to be perfect. The guest whose line was out hunched over with him helpfully, getting in the way, while the other guest, still fishing, sat back with his feet on the gunnel and enjoyed a cigar. There was an eagle up in a tree he was keeping an eye on.

Lenny was having trouble getting the knots tied. His tongue appeared and he bent his head lower. His boat drifted back slowly, pushed by the tide. Lenny didn't have a free hand to correct it. Lenny had the line by his teeth and both hands, to keep the tension. He drifted back farther, getting closer to the tideline at the back of the hole.

"Those eagles," the man smoking the cigar thought aloud, "that sure is a magnificent bird." He took another pull on his cigar, letting the smoke out slowly, and it rose in the air, languidly, like the water that flowed below it. The whirlpool chose that moment to yawn open.

When your stern drops into a whirlpool, the sensation in the pit of your stomach is similar to what you feel when dropping in an elevator. It's not that unpleasant, but when your boat starts to spin around, the feeling is quickly drowned in a host of other concerns.

When something happens at sea, from catching a big fish to sinking, it is important to remain calm. Terror tends to get in the way of clear thinking. Unfortunately, Lenny couldn't get past his initial panic. His first impulse was to jump up, run to the bow of the boat, and break out the life jackets. A good impulse, but when he got amidships he was seized by another good impulse, to run back to the motors and start up the big one. This was such a good idea that he took a couple of steps back to the stern. He saw water rising above the transom and the impulse to get to the life jackets took over again. On the way there he looked up and saw exactly where he was. The impulse to start the big engine and get the hell out of there reasserted itself. His panic had frozen the decision-making area of his brain, and he dithered ineffectually, hopping from one foot to the other in the middle of the boat. From the other boats it looked like he was doing a little dance—a whirlpool jig as he was disappearing into one.

Lenny had forgotten to tell his cigar-smoking guest to reel in his line. The man, his feet still propped comfortably on the gunnel, watched his rod tip the way Lenny had showed him. The view from the boat did seem to be spinning, but he assumed Lenny had things under control—he appeared quite calm as he did a little dance to get the kinks out of his legs. Lenny had told the man earlier that the only way he was going to catch a fish was to keep his eyes on the rod tip, so that was exactly what he intended to do.

Lenny fished for the Carringtons, and Big Jake was the head guide there. When Jake saw what was happening he started his big motor immediately. He cut both his lines and was the first boat to reach the lip of the whirlpool.

Lenny's boat was whooshing around in big circles with its stern well down; his bow swung past Big Jake's as he pulled up. Lenny's crippled decision-making saw an answer to the problem. He danced up to the bow of his boat, and as Big Jake's bow swung past Lenny reached out and clamped a death grip on the gunnel. He held on with all the strength his five foot four-inch frame could muster. Big Jake circled the vortex with him; with Lenny hanging on in such an awkward manner, there wasn't much he could do. Big Jake yelled some instructions to Lenny, but Lenny's brain was past hearing. There was nothing else for Jake to do but throw his engine into reverse and try to drag them both away from the gaping water.

Jake's motor strained and churned away. The already foaming water turned to froth as the two boats slowed their rotation and Big Jake's inched backwards. Jake was attempting to pull Lenny uphill and against the suck of the water. Lenny hung on, his skinny arms shaking with the strain. He was out as far as his armpits when he began to slip; then he was out as far as his chest. He clenched his teeth and slipped out as far as his stomach. Lenny hung on grimly.

The guides in the hole, along with their guests, were all gathered around, watching in fascination. Big Jake gave the engine more power. Lenny struggled to hold on with his knees, but he slipped again. He was soon suspended in the air, his hands on Big Jake's gunnel and nothing but his feet tucked in his own boat. His whole body shook with the exertion. A small log, caught in the same whirlpool, bumped into the side of Lenny's boat. The slight jar was all that was needed to pop Lenny loose, and he fell into the water. Big Jake fished Lenny out, coughing and sputtering, and pulled him to the safety of his boat. Wet Lenny, Big Jake, and the rest of the guides paused for a moment. The thought occurred to us all at the same time—Lenny was safe, but what about his guests? We all turned as one to look at the boat whooshing around in circles, its stern still buried.

Lenny had trained his guests well. The guy with the cigar still sat with his feet on the gunnel, patiently watching his rod tip. Lenny hadn't told him to reel in, so as far as he was concerned he was still fishing. His partner was the only one that seemed to notice that Lenny had left the boat. He looked over at Big Jake's with a casual air; perhaps Lenny needed something from Jake's boat, his expression seemed to suggest. He waited for Wet Lenny's return as though nothing out of the ordinary was going on.

Luckily the whirlpool was short-lived. It closed up on itself and disappeared as though it had never existed. Big Jake took Lenny over and reunited him with his boat. Lenny told the cigar smoker to reel up. We all went back to fishing.

Lenny dealt with the aftermath by himself. There was a considerable amount of water in the boat, all gathered in the stern where it lapped about Lenny's ankles. The water would have to be removed before they could return to fishing. Lenny could have bailed the water out by hand with a bucket he kept for the purpose, but there was something decidedly unprofessional about doing it that way, and Lenny was sensitive about being seen as unprofessional. He decided to open the seacocks and let the water run out.

Like the big luxury yachts, the guide boats were also equipped with seacocks. All Lenny had to do was open the seacock and bring his boat up to running speed with the big motor, and the water would magically drain. Lenny started the big motor and headed off into Vancouver Bay.

Lenny had overlooked two things. He had forgotten to open the seacock for a start. So, with the big motor straining to lift the boat out of the water, he had to reach under his seat where the valve was located. It was right back in the very stern, and he couldn't see it or quite reach far enough. He put his head between his legs to get a better look and strained to get his fingers on it. He almost had it when his other hand slipped off the tiller arm of the engine.

At this point the other thing he had overlooked took control of the boat.

With the boat underway, the combined weight of Lenny, the motors, and about fifty gallons of water sloshing around in the stern made it highly unstable. The moment Lenny's hand lost its grip, the motor swung violently to one side. The boat and the water on board swung with it. Lenny, with his head down to reach under his seat, was ejected into the water.

Back at the Far Side we heard the distinctive snarl of an engine revving wildly out of control. There was a loud *whump* and once again we all turned to look in unison.

Lenny's guests had the boat all to themselves again. It was whooshing them around in big circles as though they were back in the whirlpool. Lenny was nowhere to be seen—the only sign of him was his cap floating in the water.

There was a moment when we all thought he must have hit the motor as he flew out of the boat. Then we heard coughing and sputtering as he surfaced beside a floating log.

Once more Big Jake was there to pick him out of the water. He caught up to the spinning boat and called out to Lenny's guests to reach back and push the kill switch to stop the engine. Once more Big Jake reunited Lenny and his boat. Afterward, all the guides agreed that such a spectacular performance deserved to be acknowledged in some way.

"Maybe the guy just likes being wet," suggested Troutbreath. And Lenny was given a nickname.

eighteen **THE BULLET TRAIN TO TOKYO**

I DIDN'T ESCAPE the dogfish entirely unscathed either. A couple of days later I was fishing the Log Dump. Named for its use as a landing for logging operations back in the thirties, it's on the same shore as the Far Side but to the north, above the Arran Rapids and farther inside the mouth of Bute Inlet. I was with two of Herbert's employees. They were large, red-faced men with a tendency to shout even in normal conversation. They moved their hands and arms about, not so much to emphasize their loud words, it seemed, but to claim territory. The first thing they did when we got to the fishing hole was offer me a pinch of chewing tobacco.

"Ya care for a chew, Dave?"

When I declined the offer they flashed me a suspicious look—a look that suggested a real fishing guide chewed tobacco. I run across this attitude all the time. I don't care one way or the other what people put in their mouths, as long as it doesn't end up all over the side of my boat. Yet many men expect certain behaviour just because they meet me in an outdoor setting. Nobody has ever explained to me what chewing the molasses-soaked leaves of *Nicotiana tabacum* has to do with catching fish. None of the books I've read have ever mentioned its importance.

I have observed that the people expecting me to chewing tobacco are always Americans; it's almost a national obsession. To them it seems you can't truly enjoy the outdoors unless you're covering it with tobacco spit. I'm quite certain it has more to do with some kind of cultural rite of passage than anything to do with fishing.

The chewing is usually accompanied by a great deal of drinking so that a constant stream of liquid is either entering or exiting their mouths. Its not like they are practised drinkers, either. Regularly they proceed to get so drunk they wouldn't be able to land a fish if they caught one. The amount of alcohol consumed must partly explain their florid complexions.

My two gentlemen soon forgot their misgivings over my refusal to chew. Soon we were joined in the hole by four more boatloads of their buddies, with whom they were quickly hollering back and forth, trading insults.

("Hey, you ugly sonofabitch! What are you doing out here?")

While also dispensing advice on fishing.

("Hey, if you piss in the water like that you'll scare all the fish away, you ugly sonofabitch!")

And making inquiries into others' luck at fishing.

("Hey, you caught anything yet, you ugly sonofabitch?")

They all dressed alike in check shirts, blue jeans, and heavy leather boots. The boots were especially interesting: the feet are delicate, vulnerable things it seems. They must be properly protected. The boots my guests were wearing were made of thick, hard cowhide. Dense lug soles gave their feet about the same ground clearance as a Jeep. There was an impressive display of buckles and straps, cinched tight to make sure the feet couldn't possibly suffer exposure. The boots looked so heavy I was concerned that if someone fell into the water, he would be dragged down feet first before he could ever get his boots off.

I noticed that both my present guests each had a small leather case attached to their belt. I believe the case held a sharp-bladed folding knife, but, again, in all the years I've taken guys like this out fishing, I've never seen any one wield such a knife. They've been wearing it, like an external appendix, for so long they've forgotten why it's there.

We were fortunate enough to catch two nine- or ten-pound salmon in the first couple of hours. My guests got very excited, and there was much whooping and hollering each time. They compared their fish with others caught by their friends in a manner and with a choice of words that suggested they were comparing something else.

"Let's see how big yours is."

"You call that big? Hell that ain't nothing but a little trouser trout. We've got bait in the tank here bigger than that little pecker."

"You put that thing in the fish box and the box won't even know it's there, you ugly sonofabitch!"

After our initial success, the fishing died down. The yelling back and forth died down, too, and we were left to talk among ourselves. There was a long silence before finally one of them cleared his throat and asked, "Say, Dave, ya do much hunting?"

I knew that my hunting experience was completely different from anything in their realm of experience. The deer on the islands, for example, were nearly tame. They would come out to feed on the apples fallen from the trees in the orchards. If you really wanted to eat one of these animals, you could walk up to it and take it out with a fish club. I knew this wouldn't be very satisfying to someone into chewing, alcohol, and big-bore ammunition.

That subject didn't go anywhere. We spent some minutes commenting on the eagles in the trees all around us; after that there wasn't much for real tobacco chewers to talk about. Fishing, hunting, and eagles in the trees were the only topics open. They fell silent. I sensed a profound boredom settle over the pair. They squirmed and sighed like bored adolescents. One of them sat hitting the knob on the handle of his reel and watching it spin. We spent most of the next hour like this, drifting from one end of the Log Dump to the other.

I was about to suggest moving to a new location when the man named Charlie suddenly became excited.

"Hey, Dave, something's pulling on my line."

His rod bent over into the water, the tip disappearing beneath the surface. We were fishing at a depth of 120 feet in over 400 feet of water, so I could eliminate the possibility of being snagged on the bottom. If it was a salmon, it was taking no run at all; it merely bent the rod and seemed to be swimming with the boat.

"Look at it pull, look at it pull my rod! That's a fish, ain't it, Dave? Whooeee, look at that."

Of course Charlie was no expert on what a fish was supposed to feel like on the end of the rod. To be honest, I couldn't tell Charlie what he had either. There was always a possibility it was a salmon, but it could equally have been any number of other things. This was what made fishing so endlessly fascinating. From long experience I had learned not to assume anything.

The line started moving away from the boat.

Whatever it was was heading for open water.

I followed it with my boat. The line began to run off the reel.

"Hey, look at this! It's running! It's taking line!"

It was a slow, steady pull, not the slashing run usually associated with a salmon. Sometimes a fish won't realize it's hooked right away. As if to confirm this it shook the line and started peeling it out faster.

"Whoooooeeee!" yelled Charlie. "Look at that thing run!"

I knew he was completely convinced he was playing a salmon, and I knew what the next question would be.

"Say, Dave, how big do you think it is?"

I'm not as superstitious about fishing as Lucky Petersen, but there are a few things I avoid. Like most of the guides, I have a horror of weighing a fish before it is in the boat. Without fail, as soon as an estimate of weight is uttered, you may as well kiss the fish goodbye. Even if the fish is exhausted and lying over on its side begging for the net, if someone says, "Look at that! It's got to be at least thirty pounds," I know in a matter of moments I'll see the hooks drift out and it will wave its tail at me as it swims away.

"I don't like to guess about things like that," I told him simply.

"You've seen enough of these, you must have some kind of idea," he insisted.

"I don't like to say anything until it's in the boat."

"The way it's pulling, its got to be at least thirty pounds, it's got to be a tyee, don't ya think, Dave?"

I knew now that this could only end badly.

"Ummm . . . try to keep your rod tip up if you can, or you'll lose whatever this is."

"I think you're trying to change the subject on me, Dave. You're not superstitious, are you?"

"You do this as long as I have, it's inevitable," I admitted.

We had caught the fish near some of Charlie's buddies. At first they hung around, yelling words of encouragement.

"Whooeeee, Charlie, fight that sonofabitch! Hey, look, Charlie's got a big one on."

"Get that little thing in the boat, Charlie, someone might see it!"

"Don't let it get a look at you, Charlie, or you'll scare the poor thing to death, you ugly sonofabitch."

Charlie's fish continued to pull us out into the inlet. One by one the other boats left for lunch. After playing the fish for almost an hour, we were the only ones left on the water and the Log Dump was disappearing in the distance. We had yet to see the fish; not only is the water deep, but the glacial runoff from farther up the inlet clouds it heavily. A fish has to be almost on the surface before you can see it.

Charlie gained line and then lost it again. He would get the fish close to the surface and then it would slowly run back out. It was more like Charlie was taking the fish for a walk. The fish was taking another run when his friend finally voiced what I had been thinking for some time.

"Do you really think you've got a salmon, Charlie? We've been playing it for a long time and we haven't seen it yet. A tyee would have rolled or something by now, isn't that right, Dave? Maybe we should forget it and head in for lunch. I'm getting hungry. What do you think, Dave?"

"I've got to tell you, I've been thinking the same thing myself."

I had to start preparing to let Charlie down easy. His face was red from exertion and excitement. Beads of sweat stood out on his forehead, and small flecks of spittle gathered in the corners of his mouth.

"Hey," Charlie yelled over his shoulder at us, "I can't believe this. We're on the BULLET TRAIN TO TOKYO and you ladies want to get off for lunch!"

I settled back into my seat. I knew we had to see this thing through to the end. I continued to follow the fish as it headed out to the middle of the inlet. The Log Dump was now barely visible in the distance, and ours was the only boat for miles. The only sounds were the water lapping at the hull and Charlie's laboured breathing. Charlie was beginning to tire; his arm shook holding the rod and the hand turning the reel was clearly cramping.

I don't know if the fish was getting tired as well (I doubted it), or if it was just getting bored with Charlie. It swam toward the surface. Charlie was able to reel in the line and the spool filled. The weight appeared just under the water.

"Hey, I can see the weight!" Charlie yelled.

His excitement was building. He frowned in concentration and gathered the line until the weight was at the tip of the rod. Whatever was on the line was only twelve feet away on the end of the leader.

"Lift the rod, Charlie. I know you're tired but you've got to lift it up."

His whole body shook with the effort. The line sang like the string of an instrument. The rod bent over double and wobbled back and forth as he strained. A grey shape took form underneath us and suddenly there it was.

It was a dogfish.

"It's a damn dogfish!"

Charlie's friend had a way of stating the obvious.

It was a dogfish—but it was a damn big dogfish, I had to say that much. It was almost five feet from nose to tail and had to weigh well in excess of thirty pounds. It was rare to see them that big.

The hooks had snagged the back near the dorsal fin. The skin is very tough, so the hooks would never pull out; but as far as the fish was concerned they were simply a nuisance.

Charlie said nothing at all. He was numb with disappointment. I cut the line and we watched the fish swim away.

Charlie and his friend were quiet on the way back to the resort. I had some idea of what would be in store for us when we got back there. They were all waiting for us on the dock as we pulled in.

"Hey, Charlie, what did you get?"

"Yeah, Charlie, what did you get? Show us the fish."

"Is it a tyee, Charlie?"

I tied up the boat and the three of us stepped out onto the dock.

"Where is it?"

"Yeah, Charlie, where's your fish?"

Charlie looked stricken. His friend kept silent out of loyalty. The rest of his friends gathered around us. They were all looking at me expectantly. They knew the guide had to tell the true story.

"It got away," I said.

Which was true, though I was leaving out a few things.

"It got away?"

"Well, did you see it?"

"Yeah, did you see it at least?"

Though the question was addressed to Charlie they were all still looking at me, none more intensely than Charlie. I felt bad for him. His bravado of earlier in the day had evaporated. I looked at the faces of his friends crowded around. They were flushed with alcohol and filled with tobacco juice. I noticed their little leather knife cases on their belts. These men all believed in survival of the fittest. They accepted it as a primal law of nature, no matter how wrong that might be; it was one of their core beliefs. Any sign of weakness and they would turn on Charlie like mink on a stunned chicken. He would be known as Dogfish Charlie for the rest of his life. Whenever they got together they would have a good laugh at his expense, and that would have been the mildest of it.

Survival of the fittest wasn't a part of my worldview. My experiences as a fisherman had led me to believe the universe wasn't quite so predictable. There was only one thing for me to do. I lied.

"We never did see it."

"Wow..."

"It must have been a big one."

"Yeah, Dave, how big do you think it was?"

"Huge," I said. "It was a tyee for sure."

nineteen **THE TROUBLE WITH FREE ENTERPRISE**

TROUBREATH WAS IN charge of the only fuel supply in forty miles. He was in reality a lowly dock boy, a gas jockey, and a member of the subgroup known as shore staff. At most of the lodges in the area it was a very menial position, subject to the whims of the owners, and looked down upon by the guides. However, Mr. Carrington didn't pay much attention to the day-to-day running of things. As long as there were no complaints from either the guests or the guides, he didn't care what happened. Other people had worked the gas float before Troutbreath, but there had always been problems, annoying little things that distracted Mr. Carrington and took him away from his work. Since his wife had hired Troutbreath, though, things had never run more smoothly.

I had to visit Troutbreath on a regular basis to keep myself supplied with gasoline. These visits were a social time, not only with Troutbreath but also with the other guides refuelling at the same time. These visits allowed me to keep up on recent events and settle any little problems that might arise with the other guides.

Troutbreath and I were so engaged one day when a tourist interrupted us. He came to the boatshed carrying a bottle-shaped package and looking for Tom. Troutbreath wore his Brad overalls and had his long hair tucked inside a cap. He smiled, took the bottle from the man, and replied, "Tom's gone to town on the freight run, but I'll put this right here where he won't miss it when he gets back."

"Make sure the bottle doesn't get left in the sun," the man advised, "it might damage the wine. It's that Château Kirwan he liked so much the other night."

"I'll move it down here then," said Troutbreath obligingly.

This was all part of Troutbreath's subterfuge. I'd never met anyone who knew more about wine, but he found it much more useful to feign wide-eyed ignorance. The tourists expected to find nothing but backwoods yokels, and Troutbreath especially didn't want to disappoint them. ·

"You get that to him, now," the man said smiling. "I really want to thank him for helping me and my wife the other day. He really saved my ass."

"Don't worry, you've got Dave here as a witness. These guides have to tell the truth, you know, or else they take away their licence."

The man clucked and shook his head. After he left I turned to Troutbreath, "Is that the one whose boat was sinking?"

"Charts," he said laconically, the one word explaining everything. "He was using a goddamn gas station road map."

Troutbreath did a roaring trade selling the proper charts of the area to inexperienced boaters. He kept a large supply of tide books and charts stashed away in the gas shed. He even had several sets of the elaborate and detailed charts describing the flow of currents in the rapids at different times of the tide. He had a chart table set up in the shed, where he kept a set spread out. He made sure they looked well used: dog-eared and coffee stained.

He was more than helpful to the endless stream of lost souls who found their way to his docks. He took them into the shed and showed them the correct charts and the channels they should take to avoid danger. Invariably they would ask to buy the charts and the priceless information they held. Troutbreath would look pained. He'd suck in his breath and blow it out noisily. These were his only set, he would tell them. Even if he wanted to sell them, which he did, he couldn't do it. To get replacements meant a trip all the way to Campbell

River. He didn't know when he'd get the chance to get in there again.

Troutbreath knew how to play it out. I had seen him turn down twenty dollars a chart. By the time he was finished with them the tourists were forking over forty or fifty US dollars a chart, and were so grateful he was invited on board for drinks and even dinner. He would come away with bottles of the best wine and liquor, along with little packets of pâté or tins of caviar. He was so wide-eyed at these wonders, these unknown culinary delights, that his hosts were only too happy to load him up. Troutbreath had one of the finest wine cellars I had ever seen, and a pantry full of accompaniments. Considering he was buying the charts for a buck each from the Queen's Printer, he was turning a profit that would make even a billionaire blush.

"You ever get any complaints?" I asked him once.

"No, no unsatisfied customers yet," he said. He went on to explain. "Don't forget it's their idea to buy them in the first place. I do my best to talk them out of it. They set the price and even throw in the tip. They think they're bringing civilization to the ignorant locals, and who am I to tell them otherwise. And don't forget the power of the rapids—they've seen the rapids and it gets them, ummm . . . motivated. Free enterprise would go nowhere without motivated buyers. That's what these guys are. Besides, if they ever did want to find the guy who sold them the charts, the chances are only one in four they'll find him." He winked.

"No, the main problem I have is being too successful. I'm selling so many sets of charts it's taking up all my free time getting them to look just right. Giving them the right antique quality takes so much time I don't have any left to get out fishing, and it sucks."

twenty

THE TROUBLE WITH WET LENNY

"OH, BY THE WAY, I almost forgot," said Troutbreath, "I wanted to ask if you were available to guide mid-week."

Troutbreath was able to send quite a bit of work my way. The house guides at the Carringtons' were usually kept busy with fly-in guests. If all the house guides were busy, Troutbreath had to hire independents for the people on the yachts. I always tried to keep him happy.

"I've just had a mid-week cancellation. Maybe I can do it for you."

"These people have been up here once before. It's a big yacht out of Vancouver and they want to start using the resort on a regular basis, mostly family trips. They're really nice people and the boat owner is a good tipper. Could mean lots more hours if you want them."

"Sounds perfect, when do I start?"

Steady business, nice people, and good tips sounded almost too good; there had to be a catch.

"There's one small catch."

There it was. I had experienced Troutbreath's small catches in the past.

"And what would that be?"

"When they were up here last time they went fishing with one of the resort guides and they requested him again."

"And it was?"

I had a feeling I knew the answer already.

"How do you feel about fishing with Wet Lenny?"

There was a time when I felt sorry for Wet Lenny. When I first noticed him working at the Carringtons' as a rookie, he seemed shunned by the rest of the guides. I often saw him eating alone or with the shore staff. As the season passed even some of the independent guides started treating him the same way.

Lucky Petersen had such an aversion to Lenny he would jump in the bushes if he saw him approaching. I had to find out for myself what the problem was. One day in the pub I started up a conversation. This was a mistake. Wet Lenny was so happy to have a guide to talk to he took it to heart. He wanted to be my friend. He wanted to hang out, go fishing together, pal around. It wasn't long before I was joining Lucky Petersen in the bushes.

The trouble with Wet Lenny wasn't that he kept parting company with his boat. It wasn't that he mumbled when he talked, or even that he had a habit of fiddling with his mustache. The trouble with Wet Lenny—the problem that drove the guides away, caused them to jump behind the nearest bushes when they saw him coming, that left him mumbling on and on to unsuspecting shore staff or sitting alone making endless notes in a loose-leaf binder—was that all Wet Lenny wanted to talk about, the only thing on his mind, was fishing.

Wet Lenny could tell you in great detail about every fish he had ever caught. He could tell you where, when, how, and worst of all *why*. It wasn't as though these were big fish, tyees that put up memorably epic battles. He seldom caught a salmon over twenty pounds, though he didn't seem all that concerned with the quality of the fish he caught. They were just so much raw data for him.

Our conversation at the pub went something like this:

"Hey, Lenny, how big was that fish you caught at the Log Dump this morning?"

"Ummm . . . not quite twelve pounds," he mumbled, "almost a 'smiley' but not quite, missed it by three-quarters of a pound."

A smiley is what the commercial fishermen call a fish over twelve pounds. Salmon this size are sold to restaurants or caterers through a specialty market and earn more per pound. A tyee was beyond Lenny's imagination, although for Lenny every fish he caught was like a tyee, you could say that much in his favour.

"Nice spring though," Lenny continued, "had that funny little yellow spot under the chin they get if they're from Phillips Arm. Why do you think that is, anyway?"

Lenny never waited for an answer.

"Something to do with the water there I guess, or maybe it's genetic. The fish put up a damn good fight though. My guest panicked at first, but I got him calmed down. I had the drag set about two and a third turns, could have played him longer but the hooks weren't in him very well, just hanging by a piece of skin. I could have lost it any time. I put it in the net the first chance I got. Come in sideways with its mouth open, which might have caught up if I wasn't careful..."

There was, of course, much more of this, but you get the idea by now. In a way it was quite amazing. Lenny could remember fish he had caught right back to his rookie year. He could recall the depth, time of day, hook type and size, even the size and cut of the bait he was using. He kept copious, meticulous notes and approached fishing in the most logical and scientific manner possible. He kept careful track of the tides and the phases of the moon. He used a barometer and each day at breakfast and dinner he took down the barometric pressure. Lenny was out to find the unifying principle of fishing, the thing that would make it more predictable. He was looking for a set of guiding elements that would enable anyone to catch fish. Lenny was out to find the unified field theory of fishing.

"I was trolling on the other side of the inlet for that one." He was on about another fish he had caught that day. "Doing a north-south pass over in Bear Bay. I had thirty-seven and a half feet of line out using a three-ought hook with a medium size cut-plug with a left-hand roll. I think the direction of the roll makes a difference on that side of the inlet. The salmon there come out of the left side of the river, I think that determines their orientation, you know, kind of how some people are left-handed? I think fish are even more influenced because they function on a more primitive level."

There were a number of points that were unclear here, but then I didn't get much chance to ask questions.

"Then we got a thirteen and a quarter, a nine and a quarter, and the eleven and a quarter. Except for the one we caught at the Log Dump, all of them were on the left-handed spin. Of course, none of the coho would bite on the bait, but we could see them jumping. The barometer was rising and the wind was changing to westerly..."

Wet Lenny's brain was so full of theories and stratagems to catch fish it had no room to entertain the possibility that the other guides might not be so interested. Lenny's brain certainly wasn't ready for Lucky Petersen.

Lucky was terrified of Wet Lenny. He was convinced Lenny's approach to fishing made him a toy of the Fish Gods. Just talking to Wet Lenny was enough to queer Lucky's fishing for a week. Lucky didn't believe you could interpret fishing or begin to make predictions about it, and to try was a sign of tremendous arrogance. The Fish Gods enjoyed making life difficult for people that didn't show them the proper respect, and did so with a bizarre sense of humour. Lucky explained all this and more to me one day as we huddled under some bushes waiting for Lenny to pass by.

Lenny's guests, on the other hand, were always impressed. Most of them shared his methodical approach to things. They were mostly middle management and company directors who all shared a similar worldview. They agreed there was a rational explanation for everything and encouraged Lenny in his quest, even as they caught nothing but little wimpy fish. As for Lucky Petersen, they would smile indulgently, maybe even a little embarrassed for him, if he ever shared his views with them. They didn't change their minds, either, as he hauled in monster spring after monster spring; well, he was just lucky.

Lenny, however, impressed them. The boy had a system, and systems were what they could understand. None of this mystical voodoo fishing for them; their whole life was based on a system.

There was something else that worked in Lenny's favour. Most of our guests, especially the ones who flew in to the resorts on package tours, fished only once, maybe twice, over the whole season. They would relive the memory of some thirteen-pound fish all through the winter. They would show pictures of it at cocktail parties and keep one on their desks at work. The fish would magically grow in their memories, though the guides would have long forgotten them by the time they returned.

(Guides always had to deal with some guy greeting them enthusiastically, shaking their hands, and going on about some fourteen-pound fish they caught two years before. The guide could only reply weakly, "Uh, why sure, I, uh, yeah, I remember that, it ummm ... it was a great fish! Yeah, for sure, put up a hell of a fight.")

Lenny, on the other hand, could quote the time and place, the depth, even the barometric reading that day.

twenty-one   # LUCKY PETERSEN

LUCKY PETERSEN HAD always been able to catch fish. Even as a small boy, hanging a line off a dock, he caught the biggest and the most. When he got old enough to go salmon fishing in the rapids he proved to be a natural. He never missed. He quickly began to outfish the adults he went out with. Some of them grumbled that he had a special smell on his hands that was attractive to the fish. Others said it was the funny way he put a cut-plug on his leader. But most of the adults couldn't think of anything else but that he was lucky. He was doing basically the same thing as everyone else, but for some reason the fish just seemed to jump on his line.

Lucky Petersen was favoured by the Fish Gods. But far from making him feel happy, it reduced him to jittering insecurity. He knew they were capable of changing their minds on a whim, out of nothing more than a warped sense of humour. It reduced him to obsessing over every fishing-related thing he did.

One afternoon we found ourselves behind the same bush, with Wet Lenny approaching in the distance. We talked about Lenny and Lucky's reasons for avoiding him. I also learned about some of Lucky's rituals.

"I tell ya, just saying hi to the guy will shut me down for the rest of the day. I made the mistake of talking to him at the pub once and I didn't get so much as a nibble for the next three days. I've never gone that long without catching a fish in my life. Oh, he's a jinx all right. He doesn't even realize what he's doing. That's what makes him so dangerous. If he was out to bugger you up on purpose, well, you could get mad at him. But he's so damn earnest and well meaning. He really thinks that all I want to do is talk about fishing. You can't get mad at him.

"The Fish Gods have such a warped sense of humour. They're screwing with his head and he doesn't even realize it. He really thinks all them notes of his are going to tell him something. Fishing has nothing to do with graphs and pie charts. I'm sure I was a fish in a past life or something. You just have to be able to think like one. I've been catching 'em all my life and I still don't know how I do it."

Wet Lenny had passed by, but we sat under the trees and I listened as Lucky continued to talk.

"The first time I ever went guiding I was just a kid. I had this old boat . . . I'm amazed I ever went out into the rapids in the damn thing . . . I was using an old stump to sit on and my guests were sitting on a bench with life jackets under their asses to keep their butts from going numb. I didn't have a proper cutting board, so I used an old broken paddle to cut my herring on. We caught so many fish that day we were throwing back twenty-five-pounders. I still use that paddle to cut herring. It's inconvenient as hell—the herring keep sliding off cause it's sloped from the centre, but I wouldn't feel right replacing it. I still keep my bait in a white plastic bucket even though the boat I have now has a fancy built-in bait tank. I use it to keep beer cold. The white of the bucket makes the herring turn that bright greeny-blond colour like nothing else I've tried.

"But there's more to it than that. The bait tank in my boat is square, and that's not good for the energy of the herring. The herring get confused and keep bumping into the side and bashing all their scales off. It does something to them, being in a square tank. Circular, like the bucket, is much better.

"Of course, I always dip my own herring, and it's not that Troutbreath knocks all their scales off either . . . It's just . . . well, I always make sure there are an odd number of herring in the dip net and an odd number in the tank when I'm finished. Even numbers aren't good—they mess up the energy the same way squares do. I always use odd numbers. I fish at depths with odd numbers like 147 feet instead of 146 or 148. Even when I tie my leaders, I always use seven wraps on a one-ought hook."

"You use a hook that small?"

"Of course, what the hell do you use? I've seen some of these guides use a hook big enough to anchor my boat with. They don't need to be big, just sharp. But the herring is the most important part of it. If I don't feel good about the herring or I don't like the look of the way it rolls, it's gone. That voice is telling me something and I've got to listen to it. Some guests might get upset at all the time spent out of the water, but after they've caught fish with me they don't seem to care what I do.

"And these guides that let their guests hold the line or the weight, I never let them touch anything. I mean, handling the line with suntan lotion all over your hands, or even the smell of cigars ...

"Hey, did you ever see that jackass who did those videotapes with the underwater camera? You know the guy I mean—couldn't fish a doughnut out of a paper bag. He did an experiment where he dipped a herring into the bilge water—the bilge water, for Chrissakes!— and they followed it underwater to show the salmon still came after it. That's just another example of the Fish Gods having a little fun with us. They're just putting on a show for the camera to see how many idiots will actually go out and try it.

"Anyway, I never let them touch the line. You never know what kind of smell or bad energy these guys might be carrying."

"What about speculating on the size of the fish before it's in the boat?"

"Hell, no, that's the worst! That kind of arrogance is sure to be made an example of. I'll rap them on the knuckles with my fish club if they even look like they're going to do anything so disrespectful."

There was a lull in our conversation. Then Lucky Petersen added, "Spitting's good. I always spit in the water when we hook a fish. If we let it go, I spit again."

twenty-two　MR. CARRINGTON

AS I SAT in my boat at the gas dock waiting to start the party with Wet Lenny, I thought about the conversation Lucky and I had had. There was no getting around the fact that he could catch fish. I had to wonder if I would ever catch one again after being so long in Wet Lenny's company. While I sat thinking about this and other important questions, I was privileged to witness one of the rare appearances of Mr. Carrington on the gas float. That he should concern himself with the co-ordination of a fishing trip was an indication of how important the people on this yacht were.

"Who do you have working the yacht that came in this morning? The one the Brelands are staying on?" he asked Troutbreath.

"I've got Leonard and Chief on the boat," he answered. "I hope that's all right with you, Mr. Carrington."

"Oh, that should be fine, just fine."

I wasn't used to hearing Wet Lenny called Leonard; I had to think whom they could be talking about. "Chief" was another of Troutbreath's shell games; hiring outside guides was a tricky business for him, as quite often the independents were only available for one or two days before they had to start working somewhere else. Mr. Carrington hated changing guides in the middle of a party; it was one of the few things he got strange about. To get around the problem, Troutbreath started calling us all Chief. He even marked the name down on the time cards. We could use the nickname whenever

Mr. Carrington was around, which wasn't often (he never paid much attention to us or our real names anyway). Dressed in baseball hats, survival gear, and old fishing sweaters, we all pretty much looked alike to him. Just as long as the same name appeared on the time card, he didn't seem to care.

Carrington was a strange one to be manager—or owner—of a fishing resort. I never saw him go fishing, not once. I don't think he even liked fish. He never seemed to understand why people wanted to spend their time doing it. But if it made his guests happy, it also meant they wouldn't be around the resort that much. With no interruptions he could spend more time at the one thing he really loved: restoring old wooden boats.

He spent almost every waking hour in the boathouse. He'd built it for himself at the far end of the docks, as far away from the gas dock as possible. He was currently restoring a retired Fisheries patrol boat. There used to be quite a number of these boats working the coast, but the federal government replaced them with more modern and efficient vessels. The one Mr. Carrington was working on had been built in Vancouver back in the thirties. It was forty-eight feet long and put together with the finest materials available. The planking was yellow cedar laid over clear-grained Douglas fir ribs. It was finished out in teak and mahogany. All the fixtures were intact and made of heavy brass.

Mr. Carrington sanded and polished and rubbed away the years of abuse and neglect. His tall, patrician body was always covered in a light dusting of finely sanded mahogany. Under his hands the boat would come alive again. You could almost see it take new pride in its appearance. Mr. Carrington's reverence for boats afforded him a level of appreciation from the guides that made allowances for his lack of interest in fishing. They could also overlook some of his other more eccentric behaviour.

"Oh, and one more thing," Mr. Carrington yelled back over his shoulder as he headed back to his beloved avocation. "Make sure you give them the herring from the Reserve Box."

twenty-three **THE RESERVE BOX**

THE RESERVE BOX was also one of Troutbreath's innovations. All the herring used at the Carringtons' resort were netted by Troutbreath and the house guides. They rowed out at night to the front of the gas float in a specially designed skiff. Piled carefully on the stern of the rowboat was a large seine net with a very fine knotless mesh. Called a purse seine, the distinctive mesh allowed the herring to be caught with as little damage done to the delicate covering of scales on their bodies as possible. Not only did this help them live longer in the wooden holding pens, but their intact coats of shining scales made them more attractive to the salmon. Either live or cut-plugged, herring were the only bait the guides used.

The net was dropped quickly but with care as the boat was rowed in a circle around a school of herring. The purse was closed and the trapped fish carefully dipped out into the holding pens using a long-handled dip net called a brailer. Then the wooden pens were tied up near Troutbreath's office. The guides that worked for the resort got their herring for free, and the rest were sold to the outside guides and tourists.

Troutbreath didn't make much on herring, at least not compared to some of his other endeavours. Most of the money he earned there went on maintenance: the upkeep of the net, replacing tow rope and tie ups, repairs to the wooden pens (especially when they got hung on a rock in the tide), and results of storm damage in the winter. It all added up to a break-even proposition. From time to time, dogfish trapped along with the herring chewed through the mesh, and Troutbreath would have to sit down and do some careful repairs. Keeping up with the maintenance was time-consuming and didn't leave much money for the little extras like cold beer after the work was done.

Then Troutbreath hit on the idea of the Reserve Box.

Netting the herring and filling the holding pens was always done late at night. The herring were distributed among the pens indiscriminately, but only Troutbreath and the guides knew this. One night he singled out one box and put a sign on it that said RESERVED.

Troutbreath then let it be known that this box was filled with a more select choice of herring, carefully hand selected from the middle of the school and dipped only a dozen at a time to keep them in pristine condition.

The tourists were immediately interested, but when they asked Troutbreath about buying them he politely turned them down. The herring in that box were, after all, reserved.

This only made them more desirable, until the status of having bought from the Reserve Box became more valuable than the herring themselves. People started bidding the price up. They lined up with money in their hands; soon Troutbreath was selling the reserve herring, "just this one time," for more than twice the normal price. Business was so good he had to sneak down at night to switch more herring over from another box.

It was a happy solution for everybody; Troutbreath was wise enough to spend the extra money on the guides. They now had free herring and all the cold beer they could drink. The tourists believed they were getting the best herring money could buy and could even brag about how much it was costing them. Mr. Carrington heard no complaints from anybody, so he was happy.

Troutbreath was the only one less than pleased; all that sneaking around at night was one more thing cutting into his fishing time.

twenty-four **CUT-PLUGS**

A NUMBER OF people were ready to take credit for cut-plugs. Old-timers from Powell River, Campbell River, Cowichan Bay, and the Seattle Yacht Club all had claims to the distinction. It was the subject of surprisingly warm debate where fishermen gathered. There was no argument about how effective they were. The local pub kept track of all the tyees caught over the course of the summer; some were caught with live bait, but by far the majority—and certainly all of the biggest— was caught with a cut-plug.

Each guide had his own variation and insisted it was the best. Basically, the process is this. After wetting down the cutting board, a herring is singled out by hand. It's held in the left hand just behind the gills and given a squeeze by the thumb and forefinger to stun it. The head is cut off with a razor-sharp knife and the body cavity cleaned. The cut starts at the gill plate and goes from one side to the other, as well as back to front. The sharp knife cuts it cleanly, with no raggedness that would affect the spin. The two hooks of the leader are threaded through the body to make the herring spin in a straight, tight spiral. It is meant to resemble the movement of an injured herring.

Keeping the board and hands wet during the procedure helps preserve as many scales as possible, so they flash and sparkle as the bait spins through the water. The spin creates the illusion that the bait is moving like a crippled herring.

The variations are endless and subtle. There came to be a great mystique surrounding the perfection of the most effective cut-plug: a guide catching more tyees than average would be pestered by other guides for a demonstration of their technique; guides had even been known to tangle with someone on purpose, just to get a look at the way they hooked up their bait.

twenty-five **THE GUCCI LOAFERS**

WET LENNY JOINED me at the dock, but fortunately for me our party was soon seen leaving their yacht. There were four of them: the owner, his wife, and their two children, a son and a daughter. The owner struck me as a forthright and vigorous man. He shook our hands enthusiastically and introduced himself as Douglas Breland.

"But please, call me Doug."

I've noticed over the years that the people who make the greatest display of their wealth are usually the most insecure with it. Someone who feels they have to impress me with how much they have always bemuses me. What does it matter what I think? It often turns out that the guy with all the gold jewellery and the expensive and obvious watch, who has to boast about how much he has and how big his empire is worth, is either a con man or close to bankruptcy.

It's the quiet ones, the guys sporting worn flannel shirts, an old pair of jeans, and several days' beard growth, that turn out to be the serious money. The guides learn to watch for them; they are the ones who mean steady business and substantial tips.

Doug was one of these guys. If you didn't see the yacht he'd arrived on, you wouldn't pay him much attention. You might even think he worked for the resort, perhaps a gardener or something, and you might even make the mistake of asking him to do something for you. But look down at his feet—at the only thing that gave him away—his footwear.

He had on a pair of those buttery soft, buckskin-coloured Gucci loafers.

His son told me the story, after I got to know them better, of how his father had bought the boat they were on. He had been looking for a larger yacht for the family and heard this one was for sale. A wealthy and famous man had owned it, and there was a great deal of interest from people wanting to buy it. Most of them were scared off by the price, but the yacht was worth much more: the previous owner had spared no expense to outfit it and spent lavishly on the maintenance.

Doug and his son went down to the yacht club where it was moored to have a look at it. They stopped in to the sales office to make some inquiries of the agent handling the sale. They were dressed much as I have already described. Their intention was to get inside and really inspect the boat—get down in the engine room and the bilge, really poke around. That kind of inspection couldn't be carried out in a business suit or designer casuals.

However, the agent took one look at them and came to the wrong conclusion. When they asked to look at the most expensive yacht on the dock, he laughed at them and offered to show them something more in their price range. He pointed out a couple of sixteen-foot runabouts. He really thought they were joking and became quite obnoxious with these two people he thought were wasting his valuable time. The man had neglected to look down and notice their footwear.

The guy's attitude rubbed Mr. Breland the wrong way. So the very next day, with his accountant and lawyer in tow, he and his son paid the office another visit. He chose a different agent, but made sure the other one saw what was going on. He wanted the man to know who was buying the yacht and why he was losing out on a very hefty commission. He paid cash for the boat out of a suitcase full of money, like a cocaine dealer or an oil-rich Arab sheikh. He even had them throw in a sixteen-foot runabout to go on the top deck.

twenty-six **THE ENFORCER**

DOUG AND HIS wife climbed into my boat and Lenny left with the son and daughter. We stopped at the Second Hole to start. The flood tide was running strongly but fishing was slow. No bites came our way and we didn't see any fish being caught by the other boats around us. Doug and his wife, Claire, enjoyed themselves regardless, taking in the scenery and the water rushing past. The current in the channel was moving at peak speed, and the whirlpools gaped open up to fifty feet across. The boil, a severe welling up of water that formed over the reef at the downstream end of the hole, spewed water five or six feet in the air.

We were surprised to see a small inflatable dinghy leaving the shelter of Big Bay to battle its way toward the fishing hole. It was occupied by a lonely looking figure. He sat at the stern in a posture of grim determination. His hand was on an outboard motor that seemed inadequate to fight the currents. The dinghy was immediately caught in the tide and swept below the Second Hole, and the occupant had to spend several minutes gamely struggling his way back up the tide and into the fishing hole.

The boat was a bright orange that made its progress easy to follow. It reminded me of the inflatable toys made for children and swimming pools.

"As for that motor," Vop observed later when we had a chance to compare our impressions of the incident, "he would have been better off with an eggbeater."

When the guy had finally won his way back into the hole, our boat was the closest to him. He came toward us, his face fixed in a rather odd grin. As he got closer I noticed some distinctive patches on the shoulders of his jacket.

"Hello there!" he called out as he pulled up beside us.

I realized the grin was meant to put us at ease in the way of a friendly greeting; the man's terror had turned it into a grimace.

"I'm with the Department of Fisheries," he continued. "I want to check your licen—"

Before he could finish he stalled his motor trying to put it into reverse. His boat's momentum carried it into mine. It bounced off the side of my metal boat like a child's ball. The force of the collision knocked him off-balance and he fell forward onto the floor of his boat. Before he could regain his seat and start the engine he was caught by a small whirlpool. It spun his boat around like a rubber ducky caught in a bathtub drain. The centrifugal force pinned him to the floor, and he was sucked out of the fishing hole and sent off down the tide once more. This time he wasn't able to fight the tide.

We watched the bright orange boat as it bobbed slowly out of sight.

"What a curious little man," Claire remarked after he had disappeared. "What was that all about?"

"That was a Fisheries patrol officer in one of their brand new inflatables. He wanted to check our licences, you know, to make sure we weren't breaking any of the rules."

"How odd," was her only comment.

twenty-seven **THE NEED FOR EXPERTS**

THE FISHING DIDN'T get any better after the curious little man had left the hole. There wasn't any further entertainment either, so we decided to try our luck somewhere else. The tide was starting to back off, and it was the right time to run the Arran Rapids and check out the fishing at the Log Dump. Big Bay and the Second Hole are well sheltered from the westerlies that blow quite often in the summer. When we rounded the Nearside and shot through the Arrans, a strong wind from that direction was blowing across the mouth of the inlet. The wind and the tide were coming from different directions, which threw up a short, choppy sea. This made fishing the place very uncomfortable, and we were quickly soaked with a bitingly cold spray. None of us wanted to stick it out, so I suggested we try some cod fishing instead. There were some good cod holes behind the mid-channel islands, and a high slack tide was the best time to be there.

Mrs. Breland didn't want to join us on our cod expedition, preferring to get back to the yacht and a hot mug of tea. It was a simple matter to swing past it and then head across the bay.

Cod fishing is very straightforward, cod not being nearly as fussy as salmon. After you take up a position over a hole, you drop a line baited with a live herring. When it reaches the bottom you reel it up about ten feet. If the cod are there, you get instant results; if not, you simply change locations until you find them. I use a level-wind type of reel, in which a mechanism operated by a system of gears inside travels back and forth across the face of the reel and lays the line onto the spool smoothly and evenly. This mechanism can travel as fast as the line goes in or out. There is a lever that releases a brake, allowing the line to run freely off the spool. You use your thumb to control the speed of the line as it goes out. It prevents the line from creating a "bird's nest." The lever is re-engaged to stop it.

After baiting his line I explained cod fishing to Doug and handed the rod over to him. He was a bit awkward releasing the freespool lever, and the line got away from him. It raced off the reel, out of control, the level wind flying madly back and forth. Doug thrust his finger into the works to stop the line. He knew enough about backlashes but not about the reel. The finger and the level wind tried to occupy the same space, and the level wind slammed into his finger, squashing it against the side of the spool. The reel came to an instant stop. The line snapped. Doug let out a loud howl.

Doug's finger was stuck solidly in the reel. Though he was being stoic about the pain, I knew how much he must be hurting. The mechanism of the level wind can travel in only one direction; I couldn't just back it up to release the finger. I sat down with some tools and stripped the reel to extract him from it.

We did manage to catch some cod afterward, but I'm sure the throbbing in his finger must have spoiled his pleasure.

It was a quiet ride back to the yacht and we decided drinks all round were in order. Lenny returned soon after and we all gathered in the ship's lounge. Lenny had crossed the inlet and found a bay sheltered from the wind. Doug's daughter had caught a nice twelve-pound spring, and the mood of the group was elevated as a result.

After some discussion about the fish and fishing, conversation settled into a debate between Doug and his children. Doug had come out in favour of nuclear energy earlier in the day, and they wanted to argue its merits. I always try to stay out of such family discussions. I've seen them become more about the family than the topic being discussed. Old animosities surface, and as a guide I'm much better off being neutral. I sat quietly and nursed my drink. But Doug wasn't about to let me get away that easily. He turned to me.

"You're awfully quiet over there, Dave. What do you think about all this? You're a guide. You're probably sympathetic to these environmentalists."

During the course of fishing together I had learned Doug was on the boards of some major Canadian corporations. Far from providing an idle way to pass the time, the conversation might sway his opinion on any subject, which could in turn affect thousands of people. I thought about our little cod fishing adventure. Doug was sporting a bandaged finger, and only he and I knew exactly what had happened.

"I guess I have somewhat more fundamental concerns," I said, trying to be noncommittal.

"What do you mean by fundamental, Dave? This is a pretty complex issue."

There was a faintly patronizing tone in his voice. It was just enough to rub me the wrong way.

"Well, for example, I had some guy out fishing—an influential man in charge of major corporations. When a guy like that can't even operate a simple fishing reel without getting his finger smashed in the works, well, you've got to wonder what he could do if you handed him something more complicated like, say, a nuclear reactor."

Doug was quiet for a moment. I had obviously hit a sore point. He looked at me accusingly, as though I wasn't playing fair. He cleared his throat.

"Well, of course, you have to have experts to run the things."

twenty-eight  **CAROL**

CAROL HAD THE job of housekeeper at the Carringtons' resort, taking care of the cabins that the fly-in guests used during their stay. Before Carol came to the resort, the housekeeping had taken two people all day; she was able to do it by herself and finish by lunchtime. She quickly found she could more than double her income if she offered her services to the owners of the yachts at the marina, so after she'd finished the cabins each day she spent the afternoons cleaning boats. Carol was making more money in a day than most of the guides were.

Behind the resort was a trail that led all over the island. On afternoons when she had no boats to clean she could walk the trail to the lake, or, in the opposite direction, be at our house in a matter of minutes. If we were out fishing, which was often the case, she was welcome to make herself at home. Our house became a haven for her.

The indifference people showed to her comings and goings as she cleaned up after them completely amazed her. She was ready to accept most of the men as incredibly untidy. She was even willing to deal with their thoughtless demands as part of the job. She was not ready for the way people totally ignored her presence. Growing up in a small town she was always treated as an individual. No matter what you did, people recognized the person behind the job. This was definitely not true at the resort, especially on the yachts. Carol felt like a charwoman in a nineteenth-century Gothic novel. If people were on board while she cleaned, they went about their business as though she didn't exist. They would talk among themselves about the most personal matters, have arguments, even make passes at other people's wives in her presence. They would leave confidential documents lying around, open and in full view: investment plans, ad campaigns, information that would be of enormous interest to the right people.

Carol wasn't the kind of person to take advantage of the situation. Yet the way the people involved seemed to take this for granted began to disturb her. Especially when she realized their assumptions weren't based on her highly developed moral code but on the fact that she was a housekeeper. She sensed a strong condescension, even suspected they might think she was too stupid to know what she was looking at. The longer it went on the more she wanted to do something about it.

If they had taken the time to find out something about her, they would have quickly revised their opinion. As well as speaking English and French, Carol was fluent in Ukrainian and German. The Ukrainian she had learned from her grandparents and the neighbours she had grown up with in the Kootenays. This talent with language meant that her winters on the ski hills had also given her a smattering of Swedish, Italian, and even Japanese. She was also a speed-reader and her grades at college were good enough for her to win a full scholarship for the next year.

Back home Carol might have shrugged off her feelings and gone about her business. Perhaps it was hanging around with Vop and the other guides. She was becoming friends with the Brelands, so it might equally have come from hanging around with such a highly charged person as Doug. It might have been the ozone-thick air generated by the rapids. (If the rapids energize the fish that swim there, it follows that they could energize the people that live beside them.) Whatever the influence, something got inside her and she started doing things she wouldn't have done in the past. She began taking little revenges on people.

One obnoxious boat owner left her alone with a manuscript for a TV series pilot, lying open on a desk. She read through it, leaving notes and criticisms in the margins.

She wrote in German using a red pen and signed her work Fassbinder.

She wrote out a love letter in French using scented paper and left it where a cheating husband's wife was sure to find it.

Her favourite was the letter she put in the briefcase of a man she'd heard venting the most violent kind of fascist sentiments. He showed little regard for anyone the least bit different and was willing to conversationally obliterate anyone who might disagree with him. His opinions were primarily directed at anyone even vaguely descended from a Russian background. So she wrote another of her letters. This one was in Ukrainian, using the Cyrillic alphabet. It thanked the man for the useful industrial information he had passed along to the Russian consulate during his stopover in Vancouver. She left it where a secretary would be sure to find it on his return to the office.

Carol met with many quirks of human nature while she went about her job. She came to take it all in stride. One morning she found something that took her by surprise. Two guys were sharing one of the cabins. That was nothing so unusual in that the cabins were organized with that in mind. They had flown in together and appeared to be old friends, good buddies getting away for a few days of salmon fishing. They were always up first thing in the morning and off fishing before daylight. (Quite often this is a significant mark of manhood. People who sleep in past 6:30 in the morning are seen as weak and degenerate, perhaps even effeminate.) They made sure everyone knew how early they were out there.

Night found them in the lounge drinking whiskey and bragging loudly about the fish they had caught that day. They got drunk and made passes at the waitresses. Everything they did confirmed their image. They were the essence of the American outdoorsman. In check shirts and jeans, they slapped all the men on the back and called them "partner" and "ole buddy."

They were out fishing when Carol cleaned their cabin. She tidied the living area and made the beds, and then moved into the bathroom. She washed down the sink and the toilet then pulled back the shower curtain.

Carol jumped back, startled. At first she thought she was looking at a nest of long thin snakes hanging from the showerhead. Then she realized she was looking at a collection of whips, leather harnesses, bondage gear, and sexual devices. The image of the two tying each other up in mink-lined black leather made her burst out laughing. She had to sit down on the toilet seat to catch her breath. She knew if she saw them again she wouldn't be able keep a straight face, and then they would know that she knew and she didn't want to have to deal with that. Luckily they were leaving that afternoon, so she decided to have lunch over at our place and avoid the situation entirely.

The windstorm of the last couple of days had left branches strewn about the trail, and even blown down one or two trees. She picked her way along carefully, keeping an eye out for hanging branches posing a hazard above her. In a short time she stepped off the trail onto the path that led to our cottage. She found both of us home. The Brelands had flown by helicopter to see the glaciers. Vop was so exhausted from working the long hours that he had booked some time off.

"So what did you do when you found all the stuff? Did you leave another one of your famous letters?" asked Vop.

"When I finished laughing I just closed the curtains and left. These guys are regulars and I don't want them to know I found them out. Don't get me wrong, I don't care one way or the other. It's just that they're working so hard to convince everybody they're straight. I think it's dishonest. You know, I always thought the more macho a guy tried to be, the more insecure he was about his sexuality."

"I guess that means Dave and I are pretty studly guys then, eh?" said Vop sleepily.

"Tell me," I asked, "did either of them wear a little leather case on their belts, about so big?"

"I think they both did. That have something to do with it?"

"I'm not sure. It's just something I've been noticing about these macho fishermen. I haven't come to any conclusion about it yet."

twenty-nine **THE BLUE HERON**

VOP HAD BEEN working long hours. His big plan for the day was an afternoon nap on the couch. I had some errands to run, a visit to the post office to make, some guiding hours to see about, and a herring bill to pay. Carol decided a boat ride and a chance to do some sightseeing sounded like a great idea. She had been out fishing with Vop a few times and was getting more comfortable with the water. She had even run the boat for him on occasion. She had both used the small motor and driven with the big one at full speed, but only in calm water. She was still in awe of the tide. The boils and the whirlpools weren't easy to master. As yet she hadn't brought herself to run the rapids at the controls of a boat.

Once we were in the quiet water on the other side of the mid-channel islands, I let Carol take over and run the boat. We visited with Nelson and checked the mail. Nelson was in good spirits, though he was developing some kind of vision problem in his left eye. He had been to the doctor about it and done some tests, but so far they hadn't found anything obviously wrong. Maybe it had something to do with the time he spent on the water. Nelson was trying not to let it get to him, but a loss of sight was a serious thing.

We took our leave and headed back to Stuart Island, to the small bay where I occasionally bought my herring. It was just to the north of Big Bay, a few hundred yards above the Arran Rapids. During a peak tide you could hear them thunder and almost feel the pull as you stood on the herring dock.

We arrived to find Burt Asman taking care of the bait sales by himself. Burt was in his early fifties and, as his aunt and uncle would say, "a bit simple." He lived with them, and in return for his care he helped them where he could.

Burt's uncle was one of the local characters. He had been one of the first guides in the area and had hand-logged on this part of the coast for years, using the sort of equipment you can find in logging museums. He claimed the distinction of inventing the cut-plugged herring. Any fish less than thirty-five pounds he dismissed as "another one of them goddamn little feeder springs." He was retired now; he guided just occasionally and netted herring to sell to the fishermen.

Burt pointed to the shoreline on the other side of the small bay as we pulled into the dock. He had noticed a blue heron on the ground underneath the trees.

"There's a heron over on the other side there. I think it's got a broken wing. It must have happened in that windstorm we just had." Burt's simplicity didn't prevent him from showing kindness to the animals that surrounded him. "I can't leave here or I'd try to help it myself, at least put it out of its misery or something. My uncle would get mad if I weren't here and someone came to get bait. It's gonna die if it doesn't get help."

The heron has always been my favourite bird. The eagles get most of the attention, especially from the Americans, but eagles aren't much at fishing. They're really just scavengers, swooping down on dead fish floating in the water. Herons, on the other hand, truly go fishing. I would often see one standing perfectly still in the shallows along shore. It would stalk along for hours, still as the rocks around it, and then its head would dart forward into the water. More often than not, it would straighten up with a shining fish wriggling in its beak.

The eagles, meanwhile, hung out in the trees like feathered beggars.

I have observed herons through powerful telescopes and marvelled at the subtlety of their colours. Their feathers have infinite shades of grey. The ones on the wings and across their breast shine with a blue iridescence that gives them their name.

I knew there was an animal shelter in Campbell River that treated wild animals and birds. They had an arrangement with the float plane company I flew with. The scheduled mail flight would stop and pick up the bird. It could be flown back to the depot and the shelter would send someone to meet the plane. Carol and I decided to try to rescue the bird. We took my boat to the opposite shore.

While Carol held the boat off the rocks I walked up into the trees. After struggling through a fringe of thick brush, I stepped into a park-like opening under big firs. I found the bird in the clearing. One of its huge wings was obviously broken.

It eyed me warily as I approached. As I got close to it I realized exactly how big these birds really are. I stand six feet tall and the heron was looking me straight in the eye.

It thought I was getting too close and ran off up a slight rise. I followed it. Though its wing was broken its feet were working just fine, and I had to run as fast as I could to keep up with it. It dodged around trees and under fallen logs. It could hop over brush that I had to crawl through. I was soon scratched and out of breath.

I finally cornered it between a cliff face and a sharp drop-off. With nowhere to go, it turned to face its pursuer. The heron coiled its neck and prepared to defend itself with its beak. As I stood there, off-balance on the uneven ground and out of breath, I had to admit to myself that chasing the bird down was one thing—trying to capture it was an entirely different problem. The animal's beak was like a six-inch dagger that it wielded with absolute precision. With its feathered costume and *en garde* posture it reminded me of a Renaissance-era fencing master in a duel for his life: wounded but still deadly.

I walked toward it slowly, making soft calling sounds. I tried not to think about the beak or make threatening eye contact. The bird stabbed at me, recoiled, and stabbed again, but the injury and the run through the woods had weakened it. The thrusts had no snap to them. I was able to sidestep them each time. I moved closer still. The bird stabbed at me again, but again I stepped aside and then toward it. As its beak flashed past again I caught it with my left hand and hung on. The bird let out a startled squawk and struggled backwards, flapping its wings. The broken one twisted sickeningly and I was afraid it would hurt itself even further in trying to get away. Still holding the beak with my left hand, I put my right arm around its body and, cradling its wings against my chest, I lifted it up off the ground.

Now that I had the struggling bird I still had to get back to the boat. I crashed through the bushes. Without my hands to fend them off, the branches and thick underbrush slapped against my face and legs. I was covered in scratches and cuts. I managed to make it to where Carol was waiting without losing my grip on the bird. She helped me climb aboard and we sat looking at each other. The bird struggled and squawked pitifully between us. It was making strange gurgling sounds through its beak. We had to move, soon, but there was no way I could let go of the bird to drive the boat. Between home and us were the rapids, running at the peak of a sizable flood.

Carol would have to run the boat. I didn't mention how bad the rapids were at that moment; it would only make her more apprehensive. Just running the boat made her nervous enough. Running it through raging, boiling whitewater might be too much for her skill level.

We would be in the fast water almost as soon as we left the shelter of the small bay. There was a point of land between Big Bay and us. A strong riptide swirled around it, and a line of whirlpools formed downstream. Another rip formed on the opposite shore, off the mid-channel islands, and the two met in the middle of the channel in a deadly confluence. We had to pick a spot to cut through the rip into Big Bay before we were caught there and the boat flipped over.

I tried to explain this to Carol as calmly as possible, as though I was giving her directions for a drive to the corner store, but I could tell she wasn't buying it. We could hear the thunder of the water and taste the salt spray in the air. As if it could tell what we were planning, the bird began a fresh round of terrified squalling.

Carol looked pale and grim as we left the bay.

"You can do this, Carol. Watch for an opening between the whirlpools and drive the boat right through it. When you decide to make your cut, don't hesitate. It'll all be over before you know what's happened."

Maybe that was a poor choice of words.

Carol glared at me. "That's exactly what I'm afraid of."

She settled into her seat and concentrated on the water ahead.

Rounding the point was like cresting the top of a hill. The water flowed downhill into the channel that opened in front of us. Carol could see the white turbulence waiting in the middle of the channel. The spray hung in the air like steam over a boiling cauldron, while the current that swept us downstream flowed slick and smooth and travelled as fast as our boat. It gave you the illusion of slowing down even though the shore continued to rush past. In the strong current Carol lost some control over the boat. Once you were in its grip it was difficult to turn around safely, or even to steer properly. It was like entering a chute.

We passed the point and could see the line of whirlpools between Big Bay and us. They spun and writhed, opening forty to fifty feet across. The pressure of the water between them caused calm, flat spots that were higher than the surrounding water. You couldn't see what was on the other side, but if you hit them going fast enough you would fly into the air and it wouldn't matter if another whirlpool were waiting— you could fly right over it and look down into its vortex. These calm spots developed a distance below the point, and you had to wait for the right timing. At the same time Carol watched the raging currents ahead getting closer and closer. The timing was critical: the boat had to hit the opening just perfectly. The water had to be smooth. If it was all foam and air bubbles, the propeller on the outboard would spin uselessly. We would lose power and risk dropping into a whirlpool. Carol kept glancing ahead to where the water was a confusion of sucking whirlpools, pressure waves, and boils.

"Now, Carol!" I yelled as loudly as I could against the roar of the water exploding all around us. I gestured with my chin toward an opening between two huge holes.

Carol screamed and gunned the engine. She aimed the bow for the clear space. The boat hit the pressure ridge and flew into the air. We looked down into the open mouth of a whirlpool big enough to swallow the boat with indifference. Then, just as suddenly, it was behind us. The boat splashed down in a cloud of spray and foam, and Carol was soaked as a sheet of water enveloped the stern. Her scream changed as, like one of those madmen flying down the face of a snow-covered cliff face, she tilted her head back and let out a whoop of joy. We were through the rip and riding the calmer water of Big Bay.

"That was kind of fun," she yelled. She added more thoughtfully, "What are you going to do with the bird when you get it back to the house? Do you have anything you can use to hold it until they come pick it up? I mean, you can't wrestle the poor thing the whole time."

"I've got something in mind that should work perfectly."

I left Carol to tie up the boat.

The bird struggled and flapped with its good wing. I still held the beak in my left hand, the body of the bird nestled against my chest and pinned by my right arm. The sun shone down on us and I couldn't help notice the strange shadow the two of us cast on the float. It was the elongated shadow of a mythical half-man half-bird, the product of a bad dream. The shadow, the bird, and I walked up the float toward the house where Vop was still asleep on the couch dreaming the vivid, fitful dreams of the sleep deprived.

thirty **STRANGE KARMA FOR THE FRENCH PETTY NOBILITY**

"**IT ISN'T FAIR,** I tell you, it just isn't fair! That men of our station and rank in life should be subjected to such an unseemly rabble, to be scuffed and manhandled in so undignified a fashion. Why, my finest coat is a shabby ruin! This is no way for gentlemen like you and me to be treated. Someone shall pay for this when they let me out of here, of that you can be sure. I have friends in high places. I am a man of standing at Court.

"And just when things were going so well for me there, along comes this wretched business with these peasants. Well, is it any wonder that a man of refined and delicate sensibilities such as myself should be reduced to such a nervous disposition? Who in my circumstances would be able to think clearly and remain calm? Ordered about like a servant... Does this rabble really believe they can order the affairs of state? Why, they could hardly order a state dinner! What? What's that? Well, yes, I can well understand how it is possible to lose one's sense of humour in times like these.

"As I was saying ... impudent the lot of them. Parading about on the streets refusing to give way to their betters. When I condescended to address them in a vain attempt to redress their behaviour, well, they returned my good manners by laying hands on me! Indeed, they did, sir, though it passes all understanding. They taunted and used me most cruelly! My fine clothes were torn and soiled, soiled to a ruin. A well-fitted jacket or the best of cloth means nothing to these people! I was thrown into this dank and stinking cell with you. Now they've even threatened me with the chopping block—don't they know who I am?

"What? What's a *guillotine*? My good sir, now it is you who makes jests that lack wit. I couldn't think of anything more distasteful, and in front of a screaming mob of these creatures? This has to be a horrible nightmare from which I shall soon awake!"

After a few weeks in the cramped cell the French gentleman was led out, much to the relief of his cellmate. He blinked in the unfamiliar daylight. His fine clothes were reduced to tattered rags and his wig sat askew on his matted hair. He was loaded into a hay cart and paraded through the streets, which were lined with a laughing and jeering crowd. He was hauled to the square where the new invention, the guillotine, stood to receive him.

He was taken down off the cart and led up a set of stairs. The device had been erected on the top of a platform. The hay strewn about was already wet with blood. Pale and silent now, our French gentleman was strapped to a vertical board and pitched forward, his head thrust between two railings. A wooden collar was clamped around his neck and he found himself looking down into a basket. Two freshly severed heads lay in its bottom. The eyelid of one still quivered, as if giving him a ghastly wink. He heard a whistling sound and he closed his eyes. He didn't even feel the blade that sliced his head neatly from his shoulders.

When he opened his eyes again it was as if he was suspended among the lights and crystals of a chandelier—flashing and shimmering lights, great flecks of them against a blue-green void, surrounded him. He blinked and looked closer. It was hard to believe, but he was looking at a school of small fish. He was floating in the midst of them underwater. He gasped involuntarily, but instead of choking on seawater he found he could breathe quite naturally.

He looked around himself, stunned that he could breathe underwater, but he could see neither arms nor legs. He did notice something very strange: when he looked around he could see all the other fish look around as well. And he could see what they saw as they did so. He was not one of these fish—he was all of them. His consciousness, such as it was, spread through the entire school. It moved as one being. He saw what it saw from hundreds of vantage points. He felt what it felt from hundreds of tiny nervous systems. He thought what it thought, which wasn't much. His consciousness, singular and self-important to begin with, didn't go very far when spread out among so many individual beings. There wasn't much left over to wonder why he had suddenly become a school of herring.

There was so much that distracted him from thinking about what had happened to him. His many stomachs were constantly hungry. The school roamed ceaselessly looking for something to eat; the more it roamed, the more hungry it became.

As if so much hunger wasn't enough, all the other beings he came across were trying to eat him. His separate parts were in constant terror of being eaten alive. They kept up a constant, fussy complaining.

"Oh my goodness, keep moving everyone, keep moving. Don't bunch up. Keep away from those rocks! How many times do I have to tell you that's where the rock cod wait for us. Now please, keep moving . . . My God, what was that? A ling cod! A ling cod! Oh please, keep swimming up front there! It's eating us in the back!"

He felt it every time one of him was eaten—the pain of the needle-like teeth of the rock cod or the tearing of the jagged teeth of the ling cod—he felt it all, but there was always more of him to be eaten.

"Come now, let's hurry! We're getting close to that kelp bed. Oh dear, what was that?"

A silver blur streaked past the bottom of the school, eating three stragglers as it went.

"A salmon! A salmon!"

A nervous dithering cry went rippling through the length of the school. Where there was one salmon there were often many more, and they herded and terrified the herring like no other fish.

A school of herring is a nervous, darting entity. It turns and moves through the water as if it were one animal. When the whole school bunches up into a ball it acts as a kind of self-defence mechanism. The school uses so much oxygen from the water that a bigger fish, a diving bird, even a seal would lose consciousness inside the ball. Predators have learned to limit themselves to feeding on herring on the outside of the school.

However, the same thing happens to the herring if they spend too much time in the safety of the centre. They too lose consciousness and drop out at the bottom. The whole group of herring, therefore, swirls in constant motion. The herring in the centre move to the outside and trade places with those on the way back to the centre. The ones that stay too long sink to the bottom, twisting and jerking in the throes of death by suffocation. These movements are what the guides try to emulate with their cut-plugs.

Hunger brings herring closer to the surface at night. They feed on small shrimp found close to the surface after the sun goes down.

This particular evening the school rose to the surface in front of Big Bay Marina. Of course, they had no way of knowing that they were adjacent to the marina. They were simply looking for something to eat.

Troutbreath watched them come toward the spot where he and some of the guides waited, skiff and net at the ready. He tracked the movement by the gas bubbles they gave off as they rose to the surface. He waited until the whole school was in range of the net. Then he chose just the right moment to row the skiff around it while another guide dropped the net off the stern. A dim sense of panic swept through the school as the net dropped around it.

"What's this? I can't swim any farther! There's something in the way! Hey, you in the back—don't push like that! Go back, you idiots, go back!"

The school was trapped and the net was pulled closed at the bottom. The wooden pens were brought up beside the seething mass of herring and they were dipped out into them. A blizzard of herring scales filled the water (no matter how carefully they were treated, the net, the brailer, and the wooden sides of the pens always knocked off scales). Some of the herring panicked and swam straight into the side of the pens, bloodying their noses and adding to the general panic.

The nervous chatter continued through the school. There were many new things to worry about.

"Look at my coat of scales! It's a ragged mess! They've ruined me, that's what they've done, they've ruined me! I can't believe this treatment. It's not fair, I tell you, it's not fair! Being eaten by a Cod Fish is bad enough, but this is intolerable! Say, when do we eat around here?"

The herring have to settle before they can be sold as bait. They slowly calm down and begin swimming in an endless circle inside the box. They are allowed to "harden"; not being able to eat, they lose fat. The scales cling to them better and are not so easily knocked off when they are handled.

The pens are brought out in rotation, in the order they were caught, to be sold to the guides.

"Now what was that all about? Where am I now? Why, this place is even more cramped and intolerable than that last hole! Hey, you, look, I'm speaking to you up there! I demand that you release me at once, do you hear me?"

Out in the fishing hole a guide looked down at his bait tank. All the herring were standing on their tails, their heads half out of the water. Their mouths were moving frantically, as if they were trying to speak. The guide had noticed this behaviour before.

I wonder why they do that, he thought. I suppose we'll never know.

He chose a good-looking herring and reached into the bait tank. With the deft precision of long practice, he plucked it out by hand. The struggling fish was held down on a cutting board by its neck, trapped by the thumb and forefinger of one hand. The other hand was poised above, holding a razor-sharp knife.

thirty-one **THE BIRD-FEATHERED MAN**

I MADE IT to the door of the cottage, the bird still firmly in my grasp. I kicked the door open. It banged loudly against the bookcase, knocking a couple of volumes onto the floor. Vop was still asleep on the couch. His head was wedged at an awkward angle between the cushions. His feet thrashed and his mouth was moving—opening and closing like a fish starved for air. He opened his eyes sleepily.

Framed by the doorway and a halo of sunlight was a strange man-bird creature. It was making hideous, muffled squawks. It started across the rug toward him. It was about to eat him as he lay there. He flailed his arms and legs. He flipped himself backwards over the arm of the couch. He peered fearfully over it as he crouched on the floor.

A disembodied voice shouted at him.

"Hey, Vop, wake up, man, there's no time for fooling around. I need that box you keep those old outboard parts in. Can you clean it out for me, quick!"

From behind the arm of the couch Vop blinked up at me, trying to grasp what was being said to him.

"Now is the time for those engine parts . . ." the voice was yelling at him. His brain couldn't understand what this nightmare could possibly want with his old used engine parts.

Carol came in the door behind me.

"Oh, Vop, why do you always have to play around?".

She went out to the boatshed herself and returned with the box. It was tall and narrow. It had once held a small trolling motor, purchased new. Cleaned out, and with an old blanket on the bottom, it kept the bird calm and quiet, unable to move and damage its wing further.

We placed a call to the shelter and another to the airline. The plane was soon landing in front of the house.

The last time we saw the bird, the pilot was carrying it down the dock in the box. It thumped and squawked alarmingly. The poor man carried it like a bomb that was about to go off.

When Carol and I returned to the house Vop was awake enough to begin taking credit for the rescue.

"Well, it's a good thing I kept those engine parts all this time. That box would have been burned a long time ago if I hadn't. I get mocked, but it's the kind of foresight that..."

The image of the man-bird creature coming at him from out of the sun would disturb Vop's dreams for some time to come.

thirty-two  **IF A TREE FALLS**

BUTE INLET IS a forty-five-mile-long finger of water pointed at the heart of British Columbia's interior. The mountains at its mouth are relatively low, most of them around 3,500 feet. The inlet cuts through the Pacific Coast Range, and the mountains rise steadily in height as you travel its length. At its head they tower straight out of the water to a height of 10,000 feet, so that even in the middle of the summer they are still covered with snow. On the backs of the highest are the remains of the glaciers that carved out the inlet. They have been in retreat for thousands of years, and these mountains are their last strongholds, a castle keep for fading giants. Their breath is still strong enough to chill the hot summer air.

The water that fills the inlet reaches a depth of 2,500 feet. Strange ethereal creatures, some never seen by humans, live in the inky blackness. They inhabit a realm too deep for the salmon and other predators from the shallows above. They glow, a pale spectral colour of their own making. They have their own life-and-death struggles, their own predators and prey. It is a world that exists for us only in the corners of our imagination.

Shrimp and squid occupy a transitional zone, and sometimes salmon come to feed on them at a depth of 800 or 900 feet. The water above 300 feet teams with life more familiar to us, except where the fresh water of the mountain streams sits on the surface. Fresh water is like a poison to most saltwater fish. The streams that empty into the inlet turn it a bright jade green from the silt carried down due to the glaciers and the icefields. Where these creeks empty, a soft white sand is deposited along the shore.

Vop's guide boat skimmed its way across the surface of green water. The huge mountains loomed above; below, the water sank to unimaginable depths. Vop and Carol, their hair streaming in the wind, outboard at full throttle, cruised that thin line, the transition between sky and water. They were a small, insignificant presence caught up in their small concerns.

Vop's nerves were frayed. His dream of strange karma for some member of the French petty nobility, followed by his sleepy encounter with the man-bird creature, had ruined the rest he'd been trying to find. He and Carol took a day off together and decided to spend it relaxing on one of the beaches up the inlet. Carol packed a picnic lunch and Vop talked Troutbreath out of a good bottle of wine. As Vop steered the boat for the distant beach he was looking forward to spending some uninterrupted time with Carol. Finding time alone was hard on a small island, and there were things he wanted to be able to discuss with her at length.

"I get the feeling that we make her nervous sometimes," he confided in me the day before.

"Vop, you can hardly blame her. She can't even go check the mail without it becoming a life-and-death adventure."

"Well, yeah, but it's even more complicated than that. We get together and things just seem to happen. Hard-to-explain stuff. She doesn't deal very well with trips into the unknown. I'm sure she thinks it's me, but I can't explain it either. Stuff just happens, man, it's kind of spooky."

"Stuff happens to you all the time and I can't explain it either."

"You're not helping here," Vop sounded a little hurt. "Well, I'm going to make sure nothing happens tomorrow. We're going to a beach, maybe drink a little wine. If we get a sunburn that will be the worst that happens, I swear."

They left in the late morning and did a bit of fishing on the way. They trolled leisurely down the western shore of the inlet as far as the waterfall below Mount Estero. They conversed casually and enjoyed the scenery. The gnarled trees hanging onto the sheer cliffs looked like bonsai. A slight morning mist, still clinging to the trees, gave the scene the look of a Japanese brush painting.

As Vop trolled into the bright green fresh water the bait in the tank died. He and Carol decided this was the signal to reel in the lines, start the big motor, and head to the beaches. The spot they were going to was about ten miles up the inlet. The inlet narrows there, and on the western shore is a large creek that runs year-round. At the mouth of the creek are the largest of the sandy beaches. It also has one of the best views. On the opposite shore a mountain rises steeply to over six thousand feet. The ice cap on the summit glistens green-white as the sun reflects off its facets. A small creek carves a narrow path from the ice cap all the way to the sea, falling in a series of spectacular waterfalls on the way. It was the ideal setting for the picnic Vop had in mind.

Vop pulled the boat up on the sand. Together they carried the baskets and coolers to a shady spot beneath some trees where the forest came down to the beach. The sky was clear blue, without a hint of cloud, and the air was crisp and cool, a reminder of the glaciers that had created the beach.

While the scenery was awe-inspiring, there was something else that made it incredibly restful. For the first time in weeks they were completely alone, and in that solitude was silence. There were no chainsaws, no outboard motors or lawnmowers, no airplanes or helicopters taking off and landing, and, perhaps the subtlest of all, no pervasive throb of a diesel generator. Lying on the beach, they could hear the rustle of a snake as it moved through the grass behind them. They could hear the distant drubbing of a grouse, and, most startling of all, they could hear the wind rustling through the wings of a raven as it flew overhead.

Carol finally broke the silence.

"So, I'm curious, why are there two places named Church House at the south end of the island?"

"You mean Old Church House and New Church House?"

"Yeah, what's the story there?"

Old Church House is a deserted bay on the south end of Sonora Island, almost directly across from the Landing. New Church House is a small cluster of houses surrounding an old church on the mainland side of the inlet. It's nestled beneath the protection of the mountain behind it. Once it was a busy First Nation settlement; now just a few people lived there.

"Years ago," Vop began, "around the turn of the last century, the federal government wanted to settle the Indigenous people around here on the reserves they had established for them, supposedly for their own good. I think it was mainly to get them out of the way of the loggers who were starting to work in the area. They had chosen what we now call Old Church House as the site for this new village. But the people were very reluctant to move there. They weren't as enthusiastic about the idea as the government thought they should be.

"The agents for the government had a hard time understanding why. When they finally condescended to ask, the people said that the Spirit of the Wind wasn't happy with the choice. Of course, to the bureaucrats involved, good Christians all, this sounded like so much superstitious nonsense. At the time it was government policy to suppress the religion and rituals of the Indigenous people in their benevolent care. The authorities were especially freaked out by the potlatch custom. I guess there was something about the concept of giving away all your worldly goods to benefit other people that struck them as positively unchristian."

Carol remained attentive so Vop continued. "Anyway, I guess to prove the people were wrong, they went ahead and planned a whole community there. The First World War came along and slowed things down a bit, but by the twenties the loggers were all back. They forced the local people to move by making it a condition of financial aid, and they made residential school attendance mandatory. Even the church got in on it by making attendance at services dependent on where they lived.

"You'd never guess it now, but the place was like a small town when they had finished. I've seen old pictures in the museum in

Campbell River. The place had wooden sidewalks and a little dock, neat little wooden houses . . . but as good as it looked, the Indigenous people were still reluctant to move there. They still talked of the spirits and how unhappy they were.

"This only made the government work harder to move them. The church stepped up the attempt by telling them to worship God or be considered heathens. The preacher railed at them—they had to forget the old ways, the old superstitions, and enter the modern God-fearing world if they wanted to survive. You can imagine how they would have carried on. Then the government threatened to take away their children if they weren't being educated. Most of the people succumbed to the pressure then and moved there.

"The thing is, as anybody who lives here year-round knows, high winds are very common here, especially in the winter. The wind blows out of the north and then right down Bute Inlet. It funnels down the inlet and slams into the back of Stuart Island, reaching hurricane force every couple of years. That's why there are no cabins built back there. It deflects over the top of Big Bay and then comes howling across Calm Passage and hits Old Church House full on. The small valley in the back acts like a Venturi tube: increasing the speed of the wind even further. It's got to be one of the worst places on the coast for the shear strength of the wind. A few winters ago the Bute wind reached 120 miles an hour, with gusts up to 140, and it blew like that for several days.

"The first time the Bute blew, several houses in the new village were flattened and the roof of the new church was damaged. The Elders must have clucked their tongues and nodded to each other about the fury of the wind spirits. The government, not ever known for having a very poetic sensibility, wasn't going to give in easily. They rebuilt and repaired the damage. There were probably a few more sermons about heathen superstition. About three years later there was an even stronger blow that took out half the town, but still the government wouldn't give up. You know how much they liked admitting they were wrong.

"The spirits must have been having a great deal of fun by this time. They backed off for a few years, and then one winter they came raging and screaming out of the inlet. The wind blew down trees and ripped up the town. This time the wooden buildings caught fire and the whole thing burned to the ground. The poor people were left shivering on the beach in the middle of winter.

"The government finally gave in and moved the settlement across the inlet to the place where you see it now. They never did apologize or admit to making a mistake, but the people know better. New Church House is where they'd suggested building the settlement in the first place."

"None of that surprises me," said Carol when Vop had finished. "The government did the same thing to my grandparents. They came from Russia seeking freedom from persecution. The Doukhobors believed in a communal way of life. We've already discussed how those Christians felt about sharing. The government wouldn't let them educate their children their way, and they were told that their organic method of farming was spreading disease. It was all bullshit, of course—the local businessmen couldn't make any money selling them fertilizer and pesticides. They were told to adopt a more modern approach. Now everybody wants to farm organically, but so much knowledge has been lost. So many of the old people died without passing it along.

"I guess that's why I like coming to a place like this. It's so peaceful and still so wild, you can almost forget the rest of the world exists. We don't do it enough, but I guess there isn't much of an opportunity."

"We'll just have to make the opportunity. I don't have to take on as much work."

"Maybe I'm just using that as an excuse."

"What do you need an excuse for?"

"Oh, Vop, don't take this wrong, but you and your friends make me nervous."

"We make you nervous. You think we take too many chances in the tide?"

"No, it's not that simple. You guys are really careful and you all know what you're doing. It's stranger than that . . . it's hard to explain without sounding paranoid. I never know when I can let my guard down. Look at what happened the other day just going to get the mail. I don't resent rescuing that bird, but I don't know if I was ready for that much excitement. And that was just going to check the mail."

"You know I'd never do anything to hurt you."

"I know that, but it doesn't always seem to be in your control."

"Let me get this straight. You're nervous about being with me 'cause of stuff that happens that I have no control over. How can I do anything about that?"

"I'm not sure I can explain it any better. You and some of the other guides seem to be magnets for truly weird things. Things that never happen to me or anyone else I know."

"But how can I not make stuff happen that I have no control over? I don't even know why you're holding me responsible."

Carol sighed. "I don't even know why we're talking about this. I know it sounds crazy. But you have to admit, things just *happen* around you . . . it's weird."

"There is one thing I'll admit to."

"What's that?"

Vop looked at Carol. The sun shone on her hair and made her skin glow. She had lost her winter pallor, and the combination of sun and time on the water made her more attractive to him than ever. She had never looked more beautiful. A strand of hair blew across her face and Vop reached out to brush it away. He cupped her cheek in his hand and drew her face toward him as he leaned forward to kiss her.

An intense ripping, tearing sound made him stop.

Vop had heard a sound like that before; the time a tree blew down near him in a windstorm—but there was no wind, not even a breath of air. He wondered illogically if in his clumsiness around her he'd ripped a neck muscle or torn a ligament. The thought gave him a terrible turn, but the noise came again and from behind them. He turned to look. There was a large old alder tree. It stood out from the others around it and was moving toward them. It swayed for a moment as if making up its mind. Then, with a hideous shriek—a tree's final protest against gravity—it fell right where they lay on the sand.

Vop simply got up and stepped to one side, the way he might step aside for an elderly person trying to get through a door. It was a movement he made calmly as if it were the most natural thing in the world. If a tree is about to fall on you, it's best to get out of the way. Carol, however, was frozen in place. She made the mistake of taking the tree's behaviour personally. It was about to fall on *her*!

Vop reached over, took her by the hand, and pulled her beside him so calmly it was as if he did it for etiquette rather than lifesaving. He was like a father moving an ill-mannered child who remained in the way of the elderly person.

The tree slammed into the ground with a roaring crash that echoed off the mountains around them. Their blanket was driven deep into the sand by the jagged branches. Where a moment before they had been sitting and talking, there now lay a tangle of broken branches and a smashed tree trunk.

"Are you okay?" Vop put his arm around Carol protectively.

"Uh, yeah, fine. I'm fine. It'll just take me a second to catch my breath, that's all."

Carol leaned her head on Vop's shoulder. Then a thought occurred to her and she pulled away.

"How can you be so calm about this? You'd think trees were always falling on your head, no big deal! Vop, this is exactly what I was talking about. You seem to expect stuff like this to happen. I'm starting to suspect you'd be disappointed if it didn't."

"You make it sound like it was my fault."

"Dammit, Vop, I can almost believe it is! Ummm, Vop, I'm talking to you."

Vop had walked away from her to the fringe of trees. Something in the tall grass had caught his eye. He reached into a clump and pushed it aside with his hands.

"Uh, Carol, before you get too mad at me, you'd better come have a look at this."

She came over beside him and looked down at what he had found. There was a rather official looking government sign nailed to a stake driven into the ground. The sign read:

THESE TREES HAVE BEEN
SPRAYED AS PART OF

A WEED TREE ERADICATION PROGRAM

OF THE

PROVINCIAL FORESTRY SERVICES

CAUTION:

TREES MAY BE UNSTABLE
IN HIGH WINDS

PROUDLY WORKING FOR A BETTER TOMORROW

thirty-three **ROOM SERVICE**

"I **WANT TO** hear the story one more time . . . there you are on a beautiful deserted beach. You're about to kiss the woman of your dreams and a falling tree almost squashes the both of you."

"I'd rather not talk about it anymore if you don't mind."

"Are you sure you're not making this up?"

"I wish I was, but I don't have that much imagination."

"Vop, you have a totally weird and twisted imagination. Don't forget, I've seen you dreaming and it's not a pretty sight."

"You can ask Carol if you don't believe me. If she's still talking to you, that is."

"What did I do? She thinks I dropped the tree?"

"I can't even begin to explain it. I don't think she can either. Can we not talk about this anymore?"

"Whatever you say, Vop. By the way, Troutbreath wants to know if you can guide tomorrow."

"I think I need to go back to work just for a little peace and quiet. My time off hasn't been all that restful."

"The Brelands are coming up with a couple more people this time."

"That'd be cool. I hear he's a good tipper. Uhhh, I don't have to talk to Lenny do I?"

Lenny and I had been working off and on for the Brelands. They kept the yacht at the resort and commuted between it and their estate in Ladner, just outside

Vancouver. Most of their trips were made mid-week; they missed the busy weekends, which made fitting them into my regular bookings easier.

The next afternoon the three of us took them out fishing. Mr. Breland went with Vop and they returned to the dock later with a limit of sizable springs. Vop didn't go on board for drinks afterward. Later that night he expressed misgivings about guiding for them.

"I've got to talk to Troutbreath about taking me off this party," he told me as we sat at a game of dominoes.

"You guys slayed the salmon. You didn't get along or something?"

"No, it's not that, we had a great time, caught lots of fish, a great time. It's my past. It may be coming back to haunt me."

We continued our game into the night and Vop told me a long and curious tale of growing up on Cortes Island.

On the north end of the island was a beautiful and secluded cove. It had a white sand beach, protected from the wind on all sides. A cleared field visible from the beach was planted with apple, plum, and pear trees; it had once been a homestead. There was a large and well-made log house in the middle of the clearing. The house was two storeys, and the ceiling of the main living room went right to the rafters. The second-floor bedrooms opened onto an interior balcony, from which one could look down. A huge stone fireplace dominated the living room and heated the whole building. The kitchen had an antique wood stove with water coils in the firebox. They were attached to the hot water tank and supplied the kitchen and bathroom with running hot water, something of a luxury in that part of the world.

Vop had started visiting the house when he was still a young boy. Nobody ever seemed to go there and the house felt lonely to him. He would often hike the trail through thick woods and spend the day there. If it was raining, he would go inside and start a fire in the cook stove to keep warm. He loved the feel of the old kitchen, and the house seemed to enjoy his presence. The warmth kept it from deteriorating in the incessant damp.

As he got older he spent more and more time there. He collected and chopped firewood. He kept the fire stoked over the winter to keep the place warm and dry so the rot and mildew wouldn't take over. He kept the water running so the pipes wouldn't freeze and burst. He fixed the roof if the shingles were loosened by the wind. In the spring he planted flowers and herbs in borders around the house, and even a few vegetables in the garden. One year he packed in a saw and pruning tools to take care of the fruit trees.

Friends began to help him, and soon there was a group of them that spent almost all their time there, just hanging out and enjoying the peace and the hot water. The newly pruned orchard was producing so much fruit it took days to process it all. They moved in bedding and kitchen supplies as they stayed there longer. Some of them began to live there full-time. Somebody pitched a tent in the field, and a little communal scene unfolded happily and peacefully on the property.

In the warm days of summer there was no need to wear clothing. They would lounge on the beach or work in the garden getting an all-over tan. Over the years the garden was expanded and more fruit trees were planted. The people living there set up areas for candle making and weaving. They made craft items to sell at the summer fairs. A whole village was evolving in a kind of anarchic tranquility that was interrupted one day in the middle of the summer.

A Cessna float plane circled overhead and then landed noisily out in the cove. It taxied up to the beach slowly. The engine shut down and it glided to a stop in the soft sand. A man stepped out onto the pontoon.

He was an older gentleman, wearing a powder blue leisure suit with white belt and shoes. He reached back into the plane and helped a woman onto the pontoon. She was dressed in a similar manner to him, only in pink with a fluffy white angora sweater draped over her shoulders. The man helped her off the pontoon and onto the sand. With their heads down, concentrating on their footing in the loose sand, they walked up the beach toward the house.

They were so absorbed in watching where they put their feet that they almost walked right over Vop, who was sunning himself, stretched out, on a blanket. He stood up as they approached and smiled. Vop was wearing a friendship bracelet on his left wrist, an earring, a smile, and a really good tan. The man looked up, startled.

For a moment he and Vop stood there face to face, and then the woman began shrieking.

"Oh my Lord," she wailed, "oh my Lord!"

Then two more people, dressed just like Vop, walked out of the house.

"*Oh my Lord!*" she wailed again. "Oh, Harold, they're in the house!"

She brushed past Vop and went straight for the house as fast as she could over the sand. Her husband followed her.

Still shrieking, the woman disappeared inside the house. Naked people started popping out of the doors and windows, everyone trying to escape the onslaught of the crazy woman in the fluffy sweater. When she had cleared the house, she began a frenzy of cleaning.

First she threw everything she found inside the house out onto the grass.

Clothing, bedding, and other possessions were heaped together with buckets of honey and sacks of flour. Even the firewood stacked neatly beside the wood stove was thrown on the pile.

Then she began washing.

She washed the walls, she washed the cupboards, and she washed the floors and the windows. The whole time she continued to shriek at her husband. He just followed her around the house, saying the occasional "Yes, dear."

Vop and his friends collected in the woods on a hill above the house. They watched her clean. A pile of their possessions grew on the front lawn. They waited and watched all day. The woman cleaned and shrieked.

At the end of the day the house was empty but spotless. The woodwork gleamed, the paint glistened, the windows sparkled. The man and the woman got back into their airplane and took off. When the noise of the airplane finished echoing around the walls of the cove, when the house and field were silent once more, someone in the little group of stunned onlookers cleared their throat and said, "Uhhh . . . I guess that was room service."

The RCMP came by a few days later, but the possessions on the front grass and the tents in the field had all disappeared into the woods. The house sat in the clearing, clean and empty as if no one had ever been there. The police shrugged their shoulders, climbed back into their rubber boat, and left.

The people came out of the woods and slowly moved their things back into the house. They were all slightly in awe of the polished and sparkling surfaces everywhere. In a few days they were living there as though nothing had happened. Except, of course, now the windows were clean and the stove in the kitchen . . . you could see your face in it.

As far as Vop knew there were still people living there to this day.

"Well, Vop, sounds like the typical growing-up-on-the-islands-story, but what does it have to do with the Brelands?"

Vop was down to his last two dominoes.

"Bones," he said and paused thoughtfully. "Today out in the boat, you know how it goes, they were asking me where I was from, what I did in the winter, that kind of thing. When I mentioned Cortes Island he started talking about a place his parents owned there. I asked him a few questions about it, casually, like I was making conversation. He described the place. He described the log house and the cove exactly.

"Then he tells me that a few years ago his parents had a lot of trouble with a bunch of 'hippies' who had moved in there. They had to call the cops to chase them off. That's what they called us. Hippies. Like we were some kind of Charlie Manson cult. I mean, what if I said the wrong thing, or what if his parents come up here for a visit?"

"Oh, I don't think you have much to worry about there."

"What makes you say that?"

"You really think they got much of a look at your face?"

thirty-four **THE SUITS**

A FEW DAYS after Vop told me his story the RCMP docked at the gas float. I happened to be there refilling my spare gas cans. We didn't see much of them since they'd got their new boat. I watched quietly, wondering what the occasion was. Mr. Carrington made another of his rare appearances and seemed flustered and more put out than usual. There were two strangers on board the RCMP boat, and their presence seemed to be generating all the excitement.

The two men were wearing dark suits in the heat of summer. They both wore dark glasses with heavy black plastic frames. I noticed their shoes were polished to mirror brightness. They were introduced to Mr. Carrington and they shook hands all round. The small group stood on the dock, quietly talking for a few minutes. Troutbreath and I dawdled over the gasoline, straining to hear what was being said.

The Mounties climbed back aboard their boat and left. Mr. C himself escorted the two suits up to one of the best cabins, where the three of them disappeared for the rest of the day.

There followed a great deal of speculation among the guides about who these people were. Vop had watched them arrive through the binoculars we kept in the living room. We agreed on our initial observations.

"By the briefcases and the shiny shoes you'd almost think they were Jehovah's Witnesses, but the Mounties wouldn't be riding *them* around. No, they have to be cops of some kind or other."

"Mr. C was all in a sweat. Maybe they want to talk to him about something. Maybe his past is catching up with him. I've always wondered if he was hiding out—you know, like maybe he was an embezzler or he robbed a payroll truck. He's kind of a strange one to be running a fishing resort, don't you think? I mean, it's not like he's into fishing. He doesn't even seem to like making money."

There were any number of questions and even Troutbreath didn't have the answers this time. This only deepened the mystery; nothing happens on the dock that Troutbreath didn't control in one way or another. He was miffed that he couldn't find out more. Vop and I had to content ourselves with waiting until Carol went in the next morning to clean and make up the beds.

As it turned out, she was able to answer all our questions and more.

"They're cops all right, but they're American cops," she announced at lunch the next day.

"What the hell are American cops doing nosing around here?"

Vop's distrust of authority and fierce Canadian nationalism converged.

"Well, only one of them is a cop, an FBI agent," Carol continued, "the one with the blond hair. The other is from the Securities and Exchange Commission."

"What are they doing here? They're not dressed to go fishing. You think Mr. C is in trouble in the States?"

"It's got nothing to do with Mr. Carrington. As far as I can make out, some bank in Seattle got into trouble backing oil speculators from Oklahoma. The bank had to be bailed out by a takeover, but not before a lot of people lost money. It was kind of a pyramid scheme, using money from people coming in at the bottom to pay off the people at the top. It seems a few insiders got their money out in time. Some of them made a huge killing before the whole thing collapsed. They must have known what was going on."

"What are they doing up here, though?"

"Apparently the oil company kept a yacht up here. They'd entertain the investors and impress them with a real high-roller act. The suits are up here to see if they can find out what may have been discussed out fishing or in the bar at night. They got permission from the Canadian government to come here and poke around. They don't have any power of arrest or anything. They just want to ask questions and find out what they can. You might call it a fishing expedition," she concluded with a smile.

"So how do they expect to find out this information?"

"They want to talk to the guides."

"Seriously? The guides?" Vop's displeasure was growing by the moment.

"What are the guides supposed to know?"

"I guess they figure the guides might have overheard what was being talked about in the boats."

"You found all this out in one morning?"

"Well, there wasn't much for me to do while I was in their cabin. You should have seen the place. They had extra suits arranged in the closet with their shoes lined up underneath them. The beds were all stripped and the top sheets and blankets were folded and placed under the pillows."

Vop shot me a knowing look.

"Did they have all the stuff out of their briefcases lined up on a table somewhere? You know, the pencil next to the pen, the pen next to the ruler. Maybe a notepad lined up perfectly with the edge of the table? Stuff like that."

"Exactly. How did you know?"

Vop explained briefly about his roommate in college.

"You should try bouncing a quarter off that bottom sheet. I could tell what kind of mood he was in by how much height I got each time."

thirty-five **BIG JAKE**

WE DIDN'T HAVE to wait long for Carol's information to be confirmed. Big Jake, being head guide at the resort, was the first to be invited over to the cabin for a visit.

By the time he arrived Jake was well aware of what to expect. Knowing it to be an informal chat put his mind at ease. He was looking forward to the experience. After all, it wasn't every day one was interviewed by the FBI. He might even be able to have a little fun at their expense. Big Jake had developed a few techniques of his own to deal with guests that asked too many questions.

The two Americans, however, were as nervous as first-time hosts of a Tupperware party. Clearly the strength of their case would depend a great deal on what they were able to find out up here. They asked Jake to sit down and make himself comfortable. They wanted to know if he'd like coffee, and then poured one for him and politely asked what he liked in it. They offered him cake. They stressed the informal nature of their inquiries. They were here as guests of the Canadian government and would be happy with anything they could find out. He didn't have to answer any questions he was uncomfortable with. They complimented him on being the head guide and suggested that his co-operation would make it easier for them to talk to the other guides. They knew the other guides looked up to him as a leader. They flattered him for a good ten minutes. Jake knew he was being conned and was starting to get restless.

Big Jake was a friendly, helpful kind of guy. The guests at the resort all thought he was marvellous, which was why he was the head guide, and they all tried to fix him up with their daughters. Jake was polite to visitors because his parents had raised him that way; besides, he'd never found any better way to be. Yet he found he was losing patience with the transparency of these two. He finally asked them how he could be of help.

The man from the SEC sat down on the arm of the sofa and explained to Jake, in a manner more suited to a small child, that there were some bad men who had swindled poor widows out of their life savings. He knew Jake was the kind of guy that would help bring these bad men to justice. He didn't want to bore Jake with all the details, but just think how *he* would feel if somebody did that to *his* mother.

Big Jake already knew all the details from talking to Carol; he didn't find them boring at all. As for his mother, she'd lived on a farm all her life. She was a crack shot with both a rifle and a shotgun, could split firewood all day long with an axe and sledgehammer, and had once chased Larry Potts out of the chicken coop with a heavy skillet. She also had a law degree. Big Jake felt sorry for any bad men that got in her way. He didn't bother telling the SEC man any of this. Instead Jake looked down at the man's feet. Jake couldn't get over the shoes the man was wearing. The shoes looked so out of place he had to stop himself from laughing. A pair of ruby slippers wouldn't have caused him this much amusement.

The man from the FBI spoke next. He asked if Jake would like to look at some pictures, to see if he could recognize any of the people in them. Jake said he didn't mind looking at pictures at all. The tone of condescension was lost on the FBI man, who started placing a series of black-and-white photographs in front of him. Big Jake, an amateur photographer who had won prizes for his work, was appalled at the quality of the photos. Grainy blow-ups of murky shots. They looked like they had been taken through the window of a van, at a variety of locations. There were shots of men in suits standing in front of a bank. There were other photos of men in suits eating in restaurants. These were even more difficult to make out, taken as they were through the plate glass window of the restaurant as well as the window of the van.

The two men looked at him expectantly. He spent a long time looking at the pictures. He didn't quite know how to tell them. Finally he apologized to them. Even if the photography was better and you could see more of the faces, it was just a bunch of guys wearing suits. The only people Jake ever took fishing were in rain gear or check shirts and jeans. People wearing suits never went out in his boat. He had to say the photos weren't much help.

The man from the FBI looked crestfallen. He had spent months getting those photographs. It had taken countless hours in a cramped surveillance van drinking bad coffee that tasted like pencil leads mixed with chalk dust. Even now he could still taste the coffee.

The man from the SEC brightened up a little. He brought out one more photo. It was a Polaroid and showed four men squatting behind half a dozen salmon laid out on a dock. The men wore the usual shirts and jeans, baseball caps, sunglasses, and ridiculous grins.

Jake tried even harder to be helpful. He was beginning to feel bad for these guys and the kind of life they led while he was out fishing in the fresh air. He thought they didn't look all that healthy. He held the pictures close to his eyes, turning this way and that. He tried to find any distinguishing features that might help him identify the men. Finally he had to give up. They looked like all the people he had ever taken out fishing.

"I'm sorry," he said, "but you have to understand, after a while all these guys wearing jeans and check shirts begin to look alike."

thirty-six **THE DOG SALMON**

WET LENNY SPENT more and more time with the Brelands' daughter. In the evenings they would huddle with their heads together as she listened to Lenny talk about fish and his theories on catching them. She seemed pleased with the attention Lenny gave her, and so did her parents. Mrs. Breland found reasons to stay on the yacht and let the two of them go off alone.

In truth, the daughter was born into the wrong family. Where they were outgoing and thrilled by physical activities, she was quiet and bookish. They were tanned and extroverted, she was pale and withdrawn. They wore designer sunglasses, she wore corrective lenses. It was clear to see that the restless, ceaseless activity of her family most often left her a sidelined observer. With a father that dominated conversation, she had learned to listen. And her willingness to listen had left Lenny speechless—at least in the beginning. He soon got over his shyness.

One afternoon Mr. Breland announced he was going out with his daughter this time. He wanted it to sound like a fatherly desire to spend more time with his child. It wasn't hard to read between the lines: he had a fatherly desire to check out the guy his daughter was bringing home.

The fishing in the rapids had been slow lately. This suited Lenny just fine; the rapids had never been his favourite place to fish, and not only because of the danger. For Lenny's purposes they were too unpredictable to keep track of his catches the way he did. The current tossed the lines and the heaviest weights around so much he could never be sure how deep he was. He could never be sure where he was catching the salmon—and he needed to know precisely. Trolling gave him more control over the depth of his lines.

Wet Lenny headed over to the eastern side of the inlet with Mr. Breland and his daughter. Lenny had found success there often, and with Mr. Breland in his boat it was time for it to happen again. The day was oppressively hot, and Lenny was feeling the pressure.

The son and I went off in our own direction. He was tired of killing things, and given the low productivity of the fishing holes the last few days, we made the only logical decision. We would try trolling the local pub for a couple of beers.

We managed to squander most of the afternoon drinking beer and making a lazy circumnavigation of the island. We got back to the yacht to find everyone in a tizzy.

Mr. Breland had caught a big fish. From the level of excitement, I thought Lenny had guided his first tyee. I was finally able to learn the fish weighed in at twenty-four pounds: not a tyee but a respectable fish. It was also the largest fish Mr. Breland had ever caught.

Lenny was installed in the ship's lounge with a drink in his hand. Mr. Breland paced back and forth relating the struggle to land the monster. As he paced I noticed a faint squelching sound coming from his feet. I looked down.

Those buttery soft buckskin Guccis showed signs of the struggle. I got up quietly and eased away from the little group. I wanted to sneak a look at the salmon they'd caught that afternoon.

It was cleaned and stored in the freezer. When I opened it my small act of deductive reasoning proved correct.

There are five species of salmon found on the West Coast: chinook, coho, sockeye, chum, and pink.

If Vop's college roommate can create a hierarchy of the human needs, then a hierarchy of salmon is also possible. As far as the guides are concerned, the pink salmon is at the bottom. It might be seen as an evolutionary first attempt, but there are some defects. Though very numerous, they are a small, shabby fish. They never get much bigger than ten pounds, and they are so covered in slime and sea lice that the guides refuse to even touch them. At the Carringtons' resort the guides consider them a demerit fish and deduct points for keeping one. They release any they catch regardless of their guests' puzzled protests.

"No, you don't want that," the guides would say as they pitched the offending creature back into the water.

"But wasn't that a salmon?" the astonished guests would whine.

"No, it was just pretending," would often be the only explanation.

A guide—usually a rookie—hapless enough to allow a guest to keep one was awarded a demerit and was not allowed to clean it on the cleaning table with everyone else.

The sockeye salmon is really in a class all by itself. They are excellent eating but they don't feed on herring. They are almost never caught in the rapids.

The real targets of all sport fishing are the coho and the awesome chinook, which are definitely at the top of the pyramid.

The fifth species is the chum, sometimes referred to as dog salmon. They grow canine-like fangs as it comes time to spawn. The guides are rather ambivalent about the merits of this fish. Lucky Petersen has never kept one. Other guides aren't so choosy. They can get up to twenty-four or twenty-five pounds, but they are nasty, mottled things. They develop bilious-looking purple and green splotches as they get closer to spawning. The intensity of the colour in the males designates dominance, making the most colourful ones more attractive to the females. While chums can fight like an old bear on light sport fishing tackle, their bizarre eating habits taint the meat, making it stringy and tasteless. They are usually smoked and canned.

What I was looking at in the bottom of the fish cooler was definitely an example of the second-class citizen of the salmon world. As its size suggested, it was close to spawning and was a dull metallic colour with distinctive mottled stripes along its sides and huge fangs.

Chum salmon feed almost exclusively on a kind of purple jellyfish. They might strike on a herring, but it's more out of mean-spiritedness than hunger. Lenny must have dragged his cut-plug right in front of its nose. The chum bit out of anger.

I could picture the scene in Wet Lenny's boat that hot afternoon: Mr. Breland caught up in the thrill of the hunt and only seeing the fish in terms of its size—he would have been oblivious to things like species and edibility; Lenny trapped by his need to impress with no question of releasing the fish. It would have to come home and be weighed. Lenny would have no choice but to land the salmon.

The first thing a dog salmon does when it hits the floor of an angler's boat is throw up. It must be some kind of defence mechanism, like an octopus squirting ink. As Mr. Breland's chum salmon hit the floor of Wet Lenny's boat, great gouts of slimy purple jellyfish puke must have arced out of its mouth. The partially digested jellyfish produce an indelible purple dye; it stains everything it touches, forever. I know this from experience.

As I rejoined the happy group Mr. Breland was still pacing. His Guccis were now a mottled greeny-yellow-purple colour, not unlike the sides of the fish down in the cooler. Mr. B didn't seem to notice. He had caught his big fish of the summer. He squelched up and down, retelling the story of the fighting chum salmon. Over in the corner Wet Lenny and Mr. B's daughter sat holding hands. Wet Lenny had made his big catch of the summer; he had her father's approval.

I was invited to the barbecue the next day. I would have been a real shrub to turn down the invitation. I intended to sit down and eat the tough, stringy flesh of that fish. I owed it that much—Wet Lenny hadn't talked to me for days now. He had a new girlfriend, and the chum's sacrifice ensured that would continue.

thirty-seven **PITY THE MESSENGER**

I WAS ALONE in the cottage one afternoon catching up on my leader tying. The Brelands had left for their Vancouver home for a few days. Lenny, having quickly become a part of the family, had been invited to stay on the country estate. Mr. Breland had heard Lenny's theories on fish and how to catch them, and had taken a keen interest. He was convinced the guides conspired to make people think fishing was an obscure art, harder than it really was. He was sure they shrouded it so they could charge more money for their services. He felt the same way about his accountants at tax season.

My thoughts on the phenomenon of Douglas Breland were interrupted by a knock on the door. I opened it to find Gary Crane standing on the porch, a little out of breath.

"Oh great, I've found you, I've been running all over the place. I guess I just kept missing you."

"Is that so?" I hadn't left the house all morning. "I suppose you must have started looking for me over at the gas dock."

"Uh, yeah, how did you know?"

I didn't bother to answer. I didn't always want to be found, and it would be a shame to spoil Troutbreath's fun.

"So, what can I do for you?"

"Oh yeah, ummm . . . there's a boat coming in tomorrow and they want you to guide for them. I think it's Mr. Goldfarb."

As Gary was talking, my gaze wandered past him over his shoulder. Something caught my eye—a familiar Boston whaler. It was floating out past the dock, flags waving, antennae bobbing up and down as the gentle current carried it along. The boat would soon be out in the middle of the bay and headed for the rapids.

"Your dad bought some new engines, eh?"

"Yeah, he did."

"A couple of nice shiny black Mercurys."

He looked at me as though I was some kind of seer.

"We just bought those. You must have been watching me come in."

"No, but I'm watching you go out."

Gary turned to see what I was talking about.

"Hey!" he yelled, "how did that get out there?"

"Off hand, I'd say someone forgot to tie it up."

Gary looked a little sheepish as I said it.

"Uhhh . . . maybe I could have forgotten."

"They're not like horses, you know. You can't just drop the reins and expect them to stick around."

I took Gary out in my boat and we caught up to his before it could come to grief.

"Say hello to your dad for me, and tell them I'll be there to guide when the boat comes in tomorrow. And Gary, this adventure will be just between you and me."

thirty-eight **CHAIN OF COMMAND**

CATCHING A BIG fish often proves to be a curse, especially if you catch it for a guy like Morris. I seldom caught them for the right guests, the ones who lavish praise, big tips, even their daughters on the guide that catches them the big one. Some guides might catch an old dog salmon and end up being wined and dined and flown about by helicopters. I catch a tyee and all I get is a chance to go fishing with Morris again.

One of Morris's main suppliers had heard he liked to go fishing and had organized this trip. There were other customers of the company along besides Morris, and they were all being watched over by a company vice-president to make sure things went smoothly. He was vice-president in charge of something or other, a young, self-important type, what you might call "a man on the move," and he wasted no time in alienating all the guides.

"You," he said, pointing to Lucky Petersen, "are you ready to go fishing? Have you got all your bait? I hope you have enough. I don't want anyone running out of bait before it's time to come back."

He had the smell of paranoia about him.

"Listen, people"—he was walking up and down the dock clapping his hands to get everyone's attention—"make sure you all have enough life jackets on board. The water out there is pretty dangerous. You all have to be here at the dock by 5:30 precisely. We don't want anyone to be late for dinner."

"So if I'm playing a tyee, do you want me to cut it off if it's going to make us late?"

Lucky may have been teasing the VP, but then with him it was always hard to tell.

"What? What was that? If you people have any questions, make sure you know what you're doing before you leave the dock."

The mood of the guides was turning ugly. Fortunately, before the VP could be filleted by one of them, the guests appeared on the deck of the yacht.

"You," he said, pointing to me, "Mr. Goldfarb wants a Floater coat. Would you get one out of the boatshed for him."

When I returned with the jacket I was informed that I had the privilege of taking the VP and Morris out fishing. There was something in the way Morris was acting; I could sense he was even more fed up with this guy than the guides were. However, he was a guest of the man's company, an important business connection, and was doing his best to be polite.

"I think we're ready to leave now," said the VP. "Where do you plan on taking us?"

The way he asked the question suggested he wanted to approve my fishing hole selection. The guy had been here on company trips a couple of times in the past, and I couldn't help wonder how far he was willing to go offering advice. There had been good coho action in the First Hole the last couple of days, and I thought it would be worth trying again.

"Well, I was going to start off in the First Hole," I told him.

"Will we catch salmon there?" he asked blandly.

What was I supposed to say? I resisted the temptation to make a smart remark. I pulled my hat brim down over my eyes, started the engine, and pretended I was hard of hearing.

The First Hole develops just upstream from the Second Hole. A shallow reef and a kelp bed separate them. The rip forms as the tide sweeping out of Big Bay displaces the water in the channel. The water drops almost five feet as it swirls past the point, and the whirlpools are fast and vicious. They begin off the rocky point at the south of Big Bay. They are only two or three feet across, but fifteen to twenty feet deep.

Snaking past the point, they quickly open until they reach fifty or sixty feet across as they pass the Second Hole. The current in the First Hole flows continuously toward these whirlpools, and the pressure of the two opposing forces holds the rip line perfectly in place. The water is very predictable here, and one of my favourite pastimes is letting the boat slowly drift back. I like to watch my guests' eyes get wider and wider as we get closer to the line of whirlpools whispering death behind us. At just the right moment I give the small engine a slight boost and drift slowly out of harm's way.

In the early days of fishing at Stuart Island, before there were outboards to fight the current, the First Hole was one of the few places to fish. Using sleek rowboats, the anglers would row out during the slack period and stay in the eddy until the tide slacked off again.

In the thirties a platform was cantilevered out over the water and lines were dropped from it. Of course, if they caught a fish that wanted to run off down the tide, they had a problem. Even in a rowboat the fish were still fought from the back eddy. The line used was of a braided cotton that could hold a hundred pounds of pull without breaking, and the rods were as thick as pool cues. The guides look down on that kind of gear these days. They refer to anyone still using anything like it as "meat fishermen." Even with that kind of tackle, salmon broke off all the time, but there were so many in those years it didn't matter.

Outboard motors made fishing the hole less work, and a little safer, but the etiquette of the First Hole is still the same as it was in the time of the rowboats. As the tide starts to move, the boats take up positions at the edge of the back eddy along the rip. They queue up like people waiting for a bus or a movie. It's considered highly bad form to cut into this line, and no one ever does. The positions closest to the rocks off the point are considered the prime spots. If a fish is caught and it takes the guide out into the tide, the next person in line moves up into that position.

The end of the line is dangerous and an uncomfortable place to fish. The main current out of the bay hits an underwater reef and gets forced to the surface there. Called a boil for good reason, the water rises up into the air five or six feet, and covers an area as big as any of the whirlpools. A boat caught by one can be swamped in an instant. The upwelling water disrupts the consistency of the back eddy, and the boats get pushed toward the whirlpools. The guides are willing to put up with these discomforts as they wait in line.

There were only a few boats when we arrived. When big coho are in the area, the action is fast and unpredictable. I took my place in the line, put down a couple of cut-plugs, and turned my attention to holding position against the current. We didn't have long to wait.

In less than five minutes Morris's rod went completely straight and his line started to pile up on the surface. The hole is very shallow; I only had out seventy feet of line, and in a matter of seconds a huge silver-coloured shape rocketed out of the water beside our boat. It writhed and twisted above our heads on a column of foam and spray, and then crashed back into the back eddy, soaking Morris with the splash. The VP gasped. Morris looked around; he had no idea what was going on. The fish blasted out of the water again, this time on the other side of the boat. It came out beside the VP, coating his glasses with seawater and blinding him. I was already steering the boat away from the edge of the rip into the centre of the back eddy. The fish jumped again, twisting and turning more than six feet in the air. Morris still gazed about, not quite connecting the thing jumping with the action of his rod.

"Hey, Morris, stand up," I yelled at him.

"I think Mr. Goldfarb would be more comfortable sitting down," said the VP.

The coho appeared at the stern of the boat; the line came out under the hull and between the two motors. I had to do something immediately or the fish could break the light line off on the engines.

"I said stand up."

I walked to where Morris was sitting. He was still staring at the spot the fish had been two jumps ago. I grabbed him by the elbow and hoisted him out of his seat. I dragged him to the back of the boat.

"Stand there," I yelled in his ear, pointing at a spot just in front of the engines. I reached down between the outboards and released the line from where it had hung up on the engine shaft. Luckily the fish was still attached. It thrashed on the surface thirty feet off the stern.

"Now reel," I commanded him.

Morris began to reel. The coho came up beside the boat and I put it in the net. In less time than it takes to tell the story, we had a beautiful eighteen-pound coho in the boat.

Morris was ecstatic. The VP was aghast. He was looking at me with complete horror. He could hardly believe what he had just witnessed. I had manhandled Mr. Goldfarb. I had touched his eminent personage. I had dragged him out of his seat and yelled orders in his face. The man must have been seeing the Goldfarb account slipping away as he sat there.

Morris, on the other hand, was as happy as an otter in a herring crib. He had a fine, gleaming salmon lying at his feet. He liked this fishing stuff, was even starting to get the hang of it. He had stood up when I told him and he had reeled when I said reel, and the results spoke for themselves.

We went back to fishing and managed to catch a couple more coho. They weren't as big as the first one, but respectable fish and all on Morris's side of the boat. When it was time to head in he was laughing and joking expansively.

When we got back to the dock Morris invited me on board for a drink after I had cleaned the fish. Morris himself ushered me into the spacious saloon on the top deck. He invited me to sit on the couch between him and another of his fishing companions.

"What would you like to drink, Dave?" he asked me.

"Oh, a bourbon and soda would be nice, Morris."

"Say, would you get Dave a bourbon and soda," Morris said to the vice-president in charge of something or other.

"Would you like a twist with that?" Morris asked.

"Why, a twist would be lovely," I said.

"Get Dave a twist, will you? And make sure you use the good bottle."

The young VP was now in charge of the bar.

During my visit on the yacht the man sitting next to me asked what I did in the wintertime. When I told him I was an artist, a painter, he asked to see some of my paintings. I had a small portfolio with photos of my work. The next afternoon, over another bourbon and soda with a twist, he took a look at it. There was one he especially liked and he decided to buy it for his office.

"Yeah, I really like that one. Could you get it framed up, ready to hang on the wall?"

I told him there was no problem putting it in a frame. To make transporting it easier, however, it was best to leave the glass out and get a piece cut when the painting arrived. Otherwise there was the danger that the glass might break and damage the painting. Jack (I was now on a first-name basis with everybody) agreed this was a good idea. He commended me on my attention to detail.

In the fall, when I got back to the city, I had the painting framed without the glass. After a couple of phone calls back and forth, Jack and I agreed on some shipping arrangements. Jack was the owner of a large corporation that had its own transportation division and a fleet of trucks. He would have the painting picked up and handled by his own people rather than trust it to anyone else.

A week or so passed and then I got a phone call. I didn't recognize the voice but the tone and manner of approach were familiar. The guy I was talking to was no doubt some regional manager, singled out by corporate headquarters for the distinction of doing a special job. This was a man who couldn't afford any screw-ups.

"I understand you have a painting?" he sounded a little confused. What was he doing phoning this nobody? "I'll be sending someone to pick it up. Is it all framed and ready to go?"

I assured the concerned voice on the other end of the line that it was all framed and ready to go. There was one thing he wasn't confused about.

"Now, I understand there isn't supposed to be any glass in the frame. I certainly hope that's what you've done. If you haven't, you'd better remove it all before you ship it. I don't want that glass breaking and causing any damage. Are you perfectly clear on that?"

thirty-nine **THE REST STOP**

THE SUMMER WAS moving along quickly. We were all working long hours, Vop more than most. His nights were apparently still disturbed by visions of half-human bird creatures lurching toward him across fields of green shag, which he blamed me for. The days were oppressively hot, with not even a breeze to relieve the heaviness of the summer heat. The fishing in the rapids where the moving water cooled the air was slow, and we were forced to go trolling.

One afternoon, after a long lunch, washed down by several beers, at the pub with his guests, Vop and his guests headed over to the opposite shore of the inlet. The water was glass calm: not a breath of wind rustled the tranquility. He put out his lines and the party trolled slowly along the cliffs that dropped straight into the water. Conversation soon trailed off as the rhythmic lapping of the water against the hull lulled them into drowsiness. Their heads nodded. Their chins sank onto their chests. With their feet up on the gunnels, Vop's two guests were soon fast asleep.

Vop struggled to stay awake. He was, after all, a highly paid professional; sleeping really wasn't an option. He took great gulps of the warm air and tried to concentrate on keeping his eyes open. He got up and paced around in the stern of the boat. As soon as he sat back down his eyes began to close again. His eyelids were so heavy he had to close them for a moment just to let them rest. His head nodded forward. He jerked it back. His head lolled back. He jerked it forward. He thought he would close his eyes for a minute—a minute, that was all—all he needed to feel better. Vop closed his eyes and promptly fell asleep.

The little trolling motor chugged along tirelessly. They trolled on up the inlet. The boat stayed on a straight and true course while the sleeping trio twitched and snored. They stirred, found a more comfortable position, and slumbered on. One of them waved away an offending fly. The boat might have puttered on for the rest of the afternoon if it wasn't for a point of land that curved toward them.

With the lines trailing out behind them they glided through the kelp bed in front of the gently sloping gravel beach. The little lurch as the boat stopped its forward motion was enough to rouse Vop. He looked around him: the boat on the beach and the lines strung out into the kelp bed behind him. His guests started to stir. It was obvious to Vop he had been asleep for some time. There was only one way to hide this fact from his customers. Vop acted immediately.

"You guys better reel up," he announced with confident authority as he stood. "We're going to stop here a moment. I've got to take a leak."

forty **IF IT'S NOT ON TV, IT DIDN'T HAPPEN**

THE YACHT WITH Morris and the others on board had just pulled away from the dock. I was washing down the fish-cleaning table when Herbert took me aside. He was excited about a new rod and reel he'd bought the day before. He wanted to show them off. The rod was a nine-foot-long Fenwick ultralight graphite for casting, the reel an Ambassadeur, special commemorative edition. The rod was light yet extremely powerful, a very expensive mix of high technology and fine workmanship. I had seen the reel before, locked away in a glass-fronted case in one of the Campbell River sporting goods stores. It was gold plated, with a jewelled movement to reduce friction and let the line run out faster and smoother. It was put together with the precision of a Swiss watch, and cost about the same. It had waited in the case, for about forty-five years, for Herbert to walk in the front door. After he left the store the owners must have closed up and gone out to celebrate.

"What are you going to do with these?" I asked him.

I was thinking about Herbert's history with expensive equipment.

"See, that's what I want to talk to you about."

Herbert wanted to see how I hooked up my cut-plugs to catch coho. He seemed to think I was doing something special when I'd caught the ones for Morris. Herbert wanted to try out his new equipment and thought it would work well on the smaller but hard-fighting coho.

—

I took him over to my boat and showed him a few things. Coho tend to like faster, more active bait. By setting the hooks a certain way the cut-plug can be made to spin in tight, fast spirals. I showed Herbert how to cut the head off at the right angle and where to place the hooks. I suggested he try his luck along the Sonora Island shore, just above Church House, a place we called the Wall. There was talk among the guides of a good coho bite there first thing in the morning.

This insider information made Herbert feel like one of the guides, and he planned to get down there by first light the next morning. Now I knew where he was going fishing, I planned to go in exactly the opposite direction.

I was back at Nelson's resort at lunchtime the next day. I told myself I'd come to check the mail and drop off my bill for guiding Morris, but really I was curious about Herbert.

I found him standing with a small group on the dock. They were listening to his tale of fishing the morning tide at the Wall. He turned around as I approached, and he looked like he'd been in a fight. He was sporting a black eye and a couple of Band-Aids on his chin.

"What the hell happened to you?" I asked him.

"I was just telling these guys about it. It was Dave here that told me to go down to that Wall place," he said to the others.

"Sounds to me like you should have taken Dave with you for protection," one of them said. It was a sly dig at Herbert; his refusal to use guides was well known.

Herbert had gone out early that morning, flags flying, his antennae glinting in the morning sun. He had done everything I had told him. He had cut the heads off the herring at just the right angle, set the hooks just so, and trolled the bait close to the surface in a way that would entice the coho. He had caught and released two small ones right away and was feeling very pleased with himself. He was thinking about coming home for some breakfast but decided to try one last herring on the chance he might catch a coho big enough to brag about.

Ernest Hemingway has been responsible for instilling some terrible myths in the American male psyche. Killing an animal is no longer about putting food on the table, but a test of one's manhood.

The next bite on his line had set the reel to screaming. The line shot off across the surface of the water and then circled round and headed back toward the boat. The fish dove and came up on the other side. Herbert had to hold the rod in one hand and lower the obstacles he had sticking up in the air with the other. He passed the rod from one hand to the other as he navigated the aerials, flagpoles, and searchlight during his struggle from one side of the centre console to the other.

But the fish kept circling the boat, and Herbert had to follow, kicking over his tackle box and tripping on the ice chest in the process.

The fish sounded and headed out into the middle of the channel. Herbert had to start the big motor to catch up with the fish before it stripped all the line off his reel.

"I tell you," said Herbert, "it was hard to do all that and still keep the video camera on the fish."

Herbert was an endless source of surprises.

"You were videotaping the whole time?"

"Oh yeah, there's some great stuff. You guys want to see it?"

Herbert and I were the only ones that went over to his cabin. We sat down in front of the big TV he'd installed and he played the tape for me. It was a curious artifact and more than a little confusing. It started off normally enough. There were the usual shots of trees, rocks, and water. Herbert's narration called attention to the eagle in one of the trees. If you got real close to the screen and squinted, you could just make out a tiny white head among the branches. Herbert also immortalized the coho he had released so people would take his word about catching them. Then the normal flow of images changed abruptly.

The camera jerked and swung around. There was a long out-of-focus shot of the floor of the boat. Herbert could be heard swearing and there was the clatter of the rod hitting the aerials and the antennae. The scream of the reel as the line peeled off was clearly audible, and then came the unmistakable sound of the tackle box being kicked over. There was another clatter as the contents were scattered and what looked like a fishing lure rolled into the range of the camera's lens.

The camera was picked up and there was a long sweeping shot of nothing but water. Herbert's narration picked up again, but his voice was excited and he was a little out of breath. He was trying to follow the line as it slashed through the water. His hand was unsteady; the lurching and wobbling pictures of water continued until I began to feel seasick. An antenna flew past the lens before the interminable shot of water was obscured by the camera getting wrapped in a flag.

The outboard could be heard as Herbert chased down the fish. He put the camera down to reel in the slack line as he chased the fish. All I could see was the back of his jacket. The fight settled down for a time, the fish on the bottom sulking and Herbert straining to lift it. There was a long, steady shot of a fishing line disappearing into the water. Herbert had caught his breath and the voiceover was calmer now, more what you might hear on an outdoor-sportsman TV program. Herbert tried to guess the weight of the fish. He thought it might be close to twenty-five pounds.

The fish finally decided to surface and the camera was put down once again. I could see Herbert in profile working the rod. The line was coming in faster and the narration was forgotten. Herbert got the fish to the surface and his face on the screen changed. His eyes opened wide and his jaw dropped; his lips were moving, but no sound was coming out. He went out of range and returned holding the net. His face was set with a look of grim determination. He was holding the rod as high as he could with one arm and it shook with the strain.

He poked around in the water with the net held in the other hand. A look of huge surprise spread across his face. There was a brief shot of him dropping his rod and grabbing for the net with both hands, and then the camera was knocked off its perch. There followed the sounds of a physical struggle, as though a fight had broken out on board the boat. The auto-focus on the camera zoomed in and out, trying to pick an image.

Then the large eye of a very angry fish filled the whole screen. I've seen really large salmon from time to time, the ones over fifty pounds. They have a look to them—a fierceness in their eyes, and their teeth could rip a man's arm off. This was one of those fish. There was no doubt that Herbert had caught more salmon than he knew what to do with.

The TV screen went dark and there was a horrible noise. The camera had been knocked to the floor and was being slammed by the fish as it thrashed among whatever else was on the floor of the boat.

"Where are you at this point, Herbert?" I had to ask.

"Well, the fish was on top of me there for a moment, but you see here? I get the camera back and get to my feet."

As Herbert rescued the video camera, the auto-focus picked up on something as it flew out of the boat. It landed in the water before the lens could quite resolve it.

"What was that?" I asked.

"Uhhh . . . that was when the fish got its tail under the rod and flipped the whole rig out of the boat."

"You lost your new rod and reel?"

On the screen, meanwhile, Herbert appeared with a fish-club in his hand and began flailing at the floor of the boat. This only managed to make the fish madder. As Herbert swung at it, he slipped on a fishing lure underfoot and fell under the fish once again. This must have been when he got the cuts to his chin and the black eye. There was a tangle of fins and legs all wrapped up in one of his flags (the American one), and then the screen went blank as the tape ran out.

"That was something all right, Herbert. That's a hell of a fish you caught. How much did it weigh? Was it over fifty pounds? Let's go down to the cooler and have a look at it."

"It's not in the cooler."

"Did you fly it in to be trophy mounted already or—"

"It got away. Just after the tape ended. I tried to grab it but it was all wrapped up in the flag and it kind of spurted out of the boat and swam away. At least I got the whole thing on tape."

"It got away? Herbert, you let it get away? Let me get this straight. The fish gets in the boat, flips your new rod into the water, destroys your video camera, gives you a black eye and slimes your flag, and then jumps back into the water. Herbert, you weren't out fishing."

"What would you call it then?

"I'd call it a mugging."

forty-one   HAVE YOU SEEN THIS FISH?

IT WAS ALL getting to be too much for the FBI agent. He and the man from the SEC had been interviewing an endless stream of guides at the Carringtons' resort. In his line of work he had interviewed terrorists, mafioso, hijackers, and bank robbers, but they had never made him feel as uncomfortable as these guides.

He couldn't put his finger on what it was. For some reason, they all kept looking at his shoes. They would come into the cabin and the first thing they would do was look down at the shoes he was wearing. One by one they would look down and then a faint grin—more like a smirk—would cross their face. It was making him feel oddly self-conscious. He felt like he was sitting there wearing ruby slippers. He had taken to hiding his feet under the table when they came in. It was irrational, but he couldn't help himself. He was fond of his highly polished, neatly tied wingtips, and some of these guides . . . well, some of them weren't even wearing shoes.

He found them a scruffy lot. With wild and wind-blown hair, most of them were younger than his son. Some of them wore jewellery and beads. They were all articulate, almost overly polite, but their politeness was beginning to get to him. And they were just too damn healthy. He was getting irritated by their tans and sun-bleached hair. He was getting sick of the faint smell of fish that was always around them. Then there were the damn herring scales. He was finding them everywhere! On the rug, the chairs—he'd even found them in his clothing and stuck to his reading glasses!

He was beginning to get really tired of this place. From the very beginning it was as if the guides already knew why he was at Stuart Island. How they knew was a puzzle. It was one more thing that added to his irritation. And it was one thing to be on stakeout in some sleazy inner city, but to be constantly surrounded by people enjoying themselves out fishing... He'd never caught a salmon in his life.

That was another thing. The guests and the people on these yachts had looked familiar to him, so he had done a little research. When the SEC guy confirmed his research he had the shock of his life. It was no wonder the con men had run their scam up here! These guys wandering around in jeans and check shirts were some of the richest men in North America. Hell—these were some of the richest men on the planet! Just on the dock that morning were eight members of the Forbes 400. He thought he had seen Morris Goldfarb on the yacht that came in for diesel. The man had just been on the covers of *Time* and *Newsweek*, and the details of a speech he'd given had been reviewed in the *Financial Post*.

He was intimidated by the power of these men. He couldn't believe he was in their company, as superficial as that sentiment was. But the guides... just the other day he'd passed one of them chewing out one of America's most important investment bankers, calling him a "complete spud." Apparently the man had lost a couple of fish that morning, so they'd come in empty handed. *And the man had stood there with his head down and taken it!*

That was the unbelievable part of it. He even apologized. He'd asked the guide for another chance! The most powerful men on the planet and they were sucking up to these guides— these *kids*—so they'd take them fishing.

He couldn't believe what he was seeing.

He felt adrift: a man lost on an unknown sea. The warmth and comfort of the land he'd left behind were just a dim and distant memory. All the things he'd once taken for granted— power, position, rank—had no meaning here.

Here you were only as important as the last fish you caught.

When it came to the investigation, the FBI man and the guy from the SEC weren't having a much happier time. They had slowly worked through their list of guides, and the response to their questions and photographs remained the same. They would trundle out their hard won photos but without any spark or pleasure in the job. They were becoming lethargic.

Carol began to notice that the sheets on their beds weren't as taut; she wasn't able to get as much height out of a quarter as she once did. They no longer offered cake.

Wet Lenny was one of the last to be ushered into the cabin. They explained to him what they wanted to do. The words were uttered by rote, and the FBI man's voice betrayed his boredom. He laid out his pictures again one by one. The black-and-white photos of men in suits meant nothing to Lenny, just as they had meant nothing to the others. The FBI man stared off into space. The man from the SEC sighed audibly.

Wet Lenny was moved by their obvious dejection. He appreciated the scientific thoroughness of their methods. He could sympathize with their inability to land the Big One. He really wanted to help them. Almost as a reflex action, a force of habit, a fish out of water moving its gills, the SEC man brought out the Polaroid of the men on the dock displaying their fish. He was a thorough man, a stickler for details; he had to conduct each interview the same way, no matter how futile.

Lenny took the photo from him. He looked at it for a long time. He held it up close, as so many had done before. The SEC man knew it was hopeless. All he needed was a tie-in, a way of proving when these guys had been here. The timeline was the important thing—who knew what, when.

He was about to thank Lenny and usher him out the door when Wet Lenny cleared his throat. "The people in this picture I'm not so sure about," he said, "but I recognize this fish."

The man from the SEC wasn't sure he had heard correctly. The guide was mumbling in a most annoying way. The SEC man strained to hear him. "You what?" he asked.

"I recognize this fish," Lenny repeated and pointed to one of the fish in the photo.

"Uhhh . . . you recognize a fish?"

The FBI agent's mouth gaped open. The man didn't want to believe what he was hearing. He had spent two weeks inside a tiny cabin interviewing guides who seemed to be mocking his wingtips. He was wasting his life taking useless photographs and showing them to smirking civilians, and now this guy was telling them he recognized a fish. What kind of a weird, twisted sense of humour did these people have anyway?

"See here," Lenny continued, "this fish is missing its adipose fin, which means it's a hatchery fish. That's the way they mark them. It's also missing part of its tail fin, probably from a seal attack. You see these scratch marks on the skin? That's where the claws of the seal scraped the salmon as it got away."

The two government agents found themselves perking up a little; at least this wasn't the usual response. They failed, however to see the relevance.

"Well, that's all very fascinating, I'm sure," said the SEC man, "but what does it have to do with what we were discussing?"

Lenny was off and running and didn't even seem to hear the question.

"I caught that one, if I remember correctly, trolling up by the waterfall under Mount Estero. I had about forty-seven and a half feet of line out with a four-ounce weight. Yeah, I'm pretty sure, I was just this side of where the fresh water comes down the inlet. I stayed in the salt water so my bait wouldn't die, eh? I was trying a—"

"Excuse me, but you can tell all this from just looking at a Polaroid of a fish?" The FBI man could already hear how this would sound back at the office, never mind in a court of law.

"Oh sure," said Lenny cheerfully, "I keep track of all the fish I catch and how I catch them. I'm trying to understand the overall principles that govern catching fish. I want to make it more of a science, do away with all the guesswork and superstition."

"That's important work, I'm sure, but we're interested in the time frame in which this fish was caught in order to place these men here at a particular time. I don't suppose you could tell us when you caught that fish?"

It was more than the FBI man dared to hope for. He had taken out a little black notebook and was making notes with a carefully sharpened pencil.

"That was last summer, about July 26 or 27—but I may have to refer to my notes, if that's all right?"

"Notes?" said the FBI man.

"You keep notes?" asked the guy from the SEC.

"Would you mind if we had a look at those notes?"

Lenny didn't know what to say. In all the years he had been writing things down, no one had ever asked to read his notes.

He went to his room in the guide shack and got out his briefcase. He spent the rest of the afternoon and much of the evening talking about the fish in the picture, the dates when he had caught them, where, and much more. He talked about the weather and the colour of the water, and even let the investigators know about the barometric pressure.

The FBI agent filled up his first notebook and opened up another. Then he filled a third. They asked Wet Lenny everything they could think to ask and then listened to his theories on how to catch fish.

Lenny was beside himself. Never before had two people been so interested in anything he had to say.

forty-two **THE RECORD**

MY SUCCESS WITH coho in the First Hole prompted Vop to take Carol fishing there the next time they had a day off together.

There were only four boats in the back eddy when they pulled in. Vop took up his position and dropped Carol's line. Vop didn't fish. He was happy just to run the boat, holding it in one spot against the current.

If you don't have to struggle against too many boats, fishing the First Hole can be almost like meditating. Vop reacted to the water without thinking. His thoughts of where the boat should sit were translated into action by hands he was not conscious of controlling. With whirlpools forming and writhing behind him, and whitewater boiling past under the hull and reflecting in his sunglasses, Vop was as comfortable as a man in a hammock.

Carol sat with her feet on the gunnel and lay back in her seat, enjoying the warm sunshine.

A guest in one of the boats beside them caught a salmon and followed it down the tide. The boat threaded its way through the whirlpools, which opened up and flattened out below the fishing hole. The guest's rod was bent double, almost touching the water, by the strength of the fish. The guide looked intense as he steered around obstacles that could engulf his boat. He yelled instructions to his guests that Vop and Carol could hear over the roar of the water. They watched the boat until it disappeared.

"Looks like they got a good one," Carol observed languidly.

"Should be some big fish around still. It's the right time of year for another monster like Herbert's."

In a way Vop hoped they didn't catch anything. He was enjoying the tranquility he felt as the water rushed past. He was happy watching Carol holding the rod, her feet up, with the incredibly turbulent water behind her. It was a suitable contrast.

Vop was still a guide, however; he couldn't sit and watch someone else catch a fish and not try improving his own luck. Vop had Carol bring her line in and change bait. He suggested she try a little deeper, so she let out an extra fifteen feet of line. Vop relaxed back into his seat and Carol put her feet back up on the gunnel.

They had only a moment's peace. The tip of Carol's rod twitched and bent down into the water in a slow tug. When Vop first noticed it he thought the line was snagged on the bottom. He told Carol to reel her line in, as the snag would have spoiled the bait. She reeled in perhaps twenty feet of line when the rod jumped in her hand.

The line started to scream out in the other direction, taking off into the rapids—into the most violent section of water. Vop got his big motor going and they followed along the inside of the riptide. Carol's reel continued to peel line; it cut through the rip and out into the main channel. Carol stood up, careful to keep the rod at the proper angle to the pulling line. She kept two hands on the rod and just watched the level wind fly back and forth.

Vop waited until there was an opening between two whirlpools and steered the boat through it. Then he gunned the engine and chased the line as Carol reeled in the slack furiously. They got close enough to catch a glimpse of the weight; then the line flew out again. But Carol was becoming an excellent angler, and Vop didn't have to waste his concentration giving her instructions. Large amounts of driftwood and other junk floated down the channel with them. Vop and Carol were kept busy dodging and dipping the rod into the water to avoid being tangled in any of it. There was too much turbulence to try netting the fish, even if they could get it beside the boat.

Vop was content to wait while he manoeuvred into calmer water. There was no need to rush, though Carol's arms were getting tired from the exertion. She shook them in turn to relieve the cramping.

Vop had avoided talking about what was on the other end of the line.

Carol, knowing the universal horror the guides all shared, didn't dare weigh the fish before it was in the boat.

Vop finally spoke up. "We should be getting a look at whatever this is soon. It must be getting tired by now."

The First Hole had disappeared in the distance. They were very close to Kelsey Point. Another riptide formed there, and very often, when playing a big fish down the rapids, it gave the fish another burst of energy.

Vop wanted to pull the fish into a calm back eddy above the point, but the fish had other ideas. The line disappeared off into the whirlpools and they had to chase it down once more.

They'd worked the fish for almost an hour, reeling the line in and watching it peel out again. The hard work of trying to get the line in before they reached Kelsey Point was all for nothing. As the line ran out once more, they could only rest and watch it go.

"My arms are really getting tired," said Carol. She wasn't complaining, merely stating a fact that affected how well she could play the fish. "I don't know how much more of this I can take."

"It's not running as hard as before. We'll be seeing it soon, I promise," Vop said, trying to reassure her.

They crossed the Kelsey Point rip and were now in calmer water. The line angled into the whirlpools, but as Carol applied pressure it began to reel in easier and head toward the boat.

"I think it's coming up. It must want to have a look at us." Vop sounded hopeful.

Carol continued to work the rod, lifting it up and then dropping the tip as she reeled in the slack.

"You're doing great! All my guests should play a fish as well as this! The leader is quite long, so you may have to lift the rod over your head to bring the fish close enough to net."

"There's the weight!"

Carol was trying to remain calm, but her voice betrayed her excitement. She reeled in the line with extra care now the fish was so close. She backed away from the gunnel and lifted the rod. Vop got the net ready.

The weight came clear of the water and touched the tip of the rod. Vop moved in front of Carol. She couldn't see what was happening as he leaned out with the net.

"Can you get it?" she asked. Her tired arms were barely able to hold the rod high enough. They shook as she raised the rod higher.

Vop peered into the water. "It's a record," he said.

"Don't say that until the fish is in the boat! Get it in the net, quick! I can't hold on much longer."

"I don't think I'll be needing the net."

"What are you talking about?"

"I mean, it really is a record."

Vop stood up holding the line in his hand. From the bottom hook of the leader dangled a 33⅓ long-playing vinyl record.

Carol stared at it in disbelief.

"What happened to the fish? What's that doing there? Oh damn it, did I lose the fish?"

Carol was suffering the acute disappointment of losing a big fish. Only someone who's been there can truly understand her frustration. "I know I had a fish on. You did too."

Vop inspected the record. The hook was caught in the centre hole and stuck tightly. Vop dropped the record back in the water. He let it sink a few feet then pulled the line. The record pivoted face-on and he was pulling against the weight of the water. It was like trying to dredge up a bucket.

"There's your fish," said Vop. "With the full force of the tide pulling on this it would act just like a fish taking line. In the calmer water it would flatten out and we could get some line back. As soon as we got into the fast water again, it took off."

"I don't believe it. It felt just like a salmon. Look at the tiny hole the hook is in. That's pretty strange, don't you think?"

Vop grinned, his eyes twinkling at her. "Stuff happens," he said meaningfully.

He lifted the record out of the water.

"See, it's even got barnacles growing on it. We must have gotten too close to the bottom and snagged it. With the tide running so hard, it's no wonder we couldn't get it up to the boat."

"We could have gotten killed chasing down a stupid record."

Carol still couldn't quite believe what had happened. Vop was turning the record over in his hand. The side that had lain on the bottom had been protected from the sea growth; he could still read the label.

"This isn't just any record. If you think catching this was strange enough, take a look at the title of the album."

Carol's mouth dropped.

"Wow" was all she could manage to say.

"Now it's starting to happen to you. I think you're becoming one of us."

"Vop, this is trying to tell us something."

"That depends on how much you want to read into it. I don't like giving things like this too much power. If you want to take this as a sign, it might mean we're doing the right thing by being together. If you're into signs that is."

Carol leaned forward and kissed him on the lips. Her eyes twinkled.

"How about we give this back to the sea?" said Vop.

She nodded.

He unhooked the record and looked at it a moment. Then he spat on it and tossed it back into the water. The two of them watched as it fluttered out of sight.

forty-three   **WHERE THERE'S SMOKE**

ON MY WAY to the Landing that afternoon I had noticed Vop and Carol out along the rip below Kelsey Point. I didn't have time to stop and talk, and besides it looked like they were playing a big fish. I didn't want to get in the way. I was guiding for the Landing the next day and needed to talk about arrangements and starting times. It would be one of my last parties of the season. I was looking forward to winding things down and maybe having the time to visit some of the neighbouring islands.

When I arrived the RCMP's new vessel was tied to the dock and a brand new helicopter, painted white and blue with the RCMP crest on its side, was sitting on the loading dock above. The crew of the boat was well known to all the guides, and I called out to see if anyone was on board. The skipper stuck his head out a side window.

"Hey, Dave, haven't seen you in a while. You ever get any running lights on that boat of yours?"

"Of course," I said, feigning indignation, "I'm so legal it's painful. You want to hear my sound-signalling device?"

"No, thanks. The last time I asked one of you guides to demonstrate he'd rigged up an air horn from an old salvage tug. I couldn't hear anything for the rest of the day. I've just put a fresh pot of coffee on. You care for a cup?"

"I've got to go up to the office for a minute, but sure, I'll be right back down."

My return for coffee was the first chance I'd had to inspect the new boat up close, and I was suitably impressed. I sat in the wheelhouse, in the skipper's custom-built, shock-absorbing seat. Properly strapped in he could maintain full speed no matter how rough the seas.

"How fast is this thing anyway? You can tell me."

"You call my boat a thing and expect me to give you classified information?"

"What are we talking here, forty-five, fifty knots?"

"I could tell you but then you'd have to be arrested for having Crown secrets."

There was something about the way he was smiling at me.

"You're serious, aren't you? You'd actually do that."

"Damn right. You'd be the first to try our little high-tech jail. I've been waiting for an opportunity."

"No, that doesn't sound like much fun."

"I could let you go for a ride in the helicopter, how does that sound?"

"You can do that?"

"Hey, I'm the law around here, aren't I? Besides, it's a new helicopter and we've never taken it up with a full load."

"That sounds like way more fun."

I took any opportunity to go flying that came along, even if it meant flying with the only law west of the inlet. We waited for the rest of the crew and the pilot of the helicopter to return to the boat.

The pilot and the young constable (he was the same age as most of the guides) were out for a short run in the police Zodiac. The Zodiac usually sat in a special cradle on the stern of the boat. The stern was designed in such a way that the Zodiac could be dropped and retrieved while the mother ship maintained cruising speed. They used the Zodiac for short patrols and checking fishing licences and the safety equipment of the boaters and sport fishermen. We talked about nothing in particular while we waited, and then I hit on a touchy subject.

"I notice you've got the engines running. Are you still trying to burn up diesel?"

"The wheels of government grind on slowly. We've filed the request forms, but they said we need to fill out a 14W/24-9c, whatever the hell that is. They were going to mail us one from

Ottawa, but that was over a month ago. We've got a similar problem with the helicopter."

The skipper enjoyed stories of official incompetence and bungling—anything that made the bureaucrats at the office look bad. He had worked his way through the ranks and had spent years of his life in isolated postings. Now he was in a senior position, he didn't mind speaking out, at least to the guides.

"They bought this new helicopter to patrol several different jurisdictions from here to Bella Bella. Each jurisdiction is assigned so many hours of flying time. Of course we have to use all of ours or we don't get as many next year. Hell, we like to go flying, so we're off again this afternoon."

The Zodiac returned before he could launch into a broader complaint about the bureaucratically inept. It was soon stowed on its cradle, and we boarded the helicopter and took off, heading south.

In a short time we were over Cortes Island. I noticed smoke coming from a log cabin nestled in a small cove on the north end of Cortes, where we swung west. The helicopter was extremely fast, and we were able to cover a great deal of territory. We flew over several spots that were well known as good sailboat anchorage, but no boats were moored in any of them. The officers seemed disappointed; they were on the lookout for something. We flew around the bottom of Reid Island and over to the Octopus Islands, another favourite spot for sailboaters. This time there were a couple of boats moored there. We circled above them.

"What are you looking for?" I asked.

"Oh, we're just, uhhh…assessing our surveillance capabilities," the skipper replied over the intercom. He was checking out the boat below with a pair of high-powered binoculars.

"You know, it looks to me like those women on the boat down there aren't wearing any tops."

"We're on official business here. That would be more classified information."

"About as official as my ass! I can't believe you guys, up here on taxpayers' money, checking out some taxpayers' breasts…"

Before I got a chance to continue we passed the moorage and turned north over Reid Island. As we came up on a low ridge, the skipper noticed something and had the pilot come around for another pass. Scattered among the salal bushes and obviously out of place were some bright green plants. The skipper got quite excited and asked the pilot to find somewhere to set the helicopter down.

He found a flat clearing not too far away and landed. Closer inspection confirmed they had found a small marijuana plantation, about thirty plants in all.

"It's a shame tearing these up now. In another couple of weeks they'd be mature."

I had to watch as they pulled the plants up.

"Well, if you ask me, I wouldn't mind if they legalize the stuff," said the skipper. "It just means more paperwork for us, and even if the growers are stupid enough to be here when we land, the most they ever get is a hundred-dollar fine."

"Why do you bother stopping at all then?"

"You mean, besides the fact it's our job? If you want to know the truth, it looks good on paper and the bureaucrats give us more time to fly the helicopter."

They found a tarp in the bushes and used it to sling the plants from the landing gear. They were quite cheerful on the ride back to the Landing and invited me to have lunch with them the next day before I started guiding.

I didn't start until 2:00, so when I showed up at noon I had a couple of hours to enjoy their lunch. It was almost ready as I climbed on board. The skipper was doing his bit as the ship's cook. They were still quite elated over their little find the previous day and were in very high spirits.

I noticed an odd but familiar odour as I entered the wheelhouse, but I couldn't quite place it. The young constable took me on a quick tour of his ship. He seemed proud of his assignment; it must have been a choice commission to receive, at least compared to being stuck in the boonies being eaten by mosquitoes, or doing traffic detail in Surrey. He showed me the automatic charting system. It worked with computer-driven imaging that plotted the real-time course of the vessel and displayed it in relation to the prepro-grammed chart information. He was like a kid with a new computer game as he showed me all the things it was capable of doing.

"Of course," he giggled, "I can't show you how this works when we're at full speed, 'cause that's classified."

He found this highly amusing for some reason and started to giggle even more.

"I'd have to arrest you." He was turning red in the face.

"Hey," piped up the pilot, "why don't you show him the cruise control?"

"This boat's got cruise control?"

"The boat doesn't, but the skipper does."

This struck both the pilot and the constable as hilarious and they both laughed so hard they started to choke.

"Hey, Dave, don't waste your time with those idiots. They haven't made sense all morning. The way they're acting, you'd think we just busted the French Connection or something. Come on down here, I want you to taste this for me."

I joined the skipper in the galley. The odd smell was even stronger here. It was very familiar to me, but I still couldn't place it.

"I just pulled these cinnamon buns out of the oven. Here, try one."

He offered me a roll and took a huge bite of one himself.

"Oh man." The skipper closed his eyes. "Isn't that the best thing you've ever tasted? They just melt in your mouth when they're fresh out of the oven like this."

He rolled his eyes and took another huge bite that nearly finished off the rest of the bun.

"My mother used to make these. The smell always reminds me of her kitchen. I used to come home from school and she'd feed me cinnamon buns."

He was talking through his mouthful. Icing clung to his lips.

"She's dead now, bless her soul, but whenever I make cin-namon buns it's like my old mum is there with me, you know? Do you ever think like that about smells, Dave?"

In all the time I'd known the skipper, he'd never talked about his mother or opened himself up so emotionally. Not that there was anything wrong with a guy talking about his dear departed mother, but there was something about the dreamy look on his face and the way he was putting away a pan full of cinnamon buns. If I didn't know better, I would have thought he was stoned.

Then I recalled where I had come across the funny odour. It became obvious why I had had such a hard time placing it in the context of being on a police boat.

"Hey, Skipper." I dropped my voice to a whisper. "Just between you and me, you guys haven't been sampling that marijuana you busted the other day, have you? I mean, strictly in the spirit of scientific research of course."

This struck the man as being extremely funny.

"Us! You think we've been smoking pot? Hell, don't you know that's illegal? Why, we'd have to arrest ourselves! A Mountie always gets himself."

He started laughing so hard he choked on the cinnamon bun. I gave him a few minutes to catch his breath.

"No, really," I said, "ever since I came on board, I've smelled smoke."

"Smoke?" he said, the responsibility of command sobering him up a little. "You say you can smell smoke?"

"Yeah, maybe you guys have been on board all morning and you don't notice it, but take my word for it, it's there."

"Smells like marijuana, you say?"

"Well, yeah, I, umm, smelled it once. A roommate in college, you know how it is."

He started laughing some more.

"Now that's funny."

"What? That I want you to believe it was my roommate who was smoking?"

"You expect me to believe you really went to college?"

He was laughing so hard now that tears were coming out of his eyes. I felt like an outsider with no sense of humour as I stood watching the man trying to regain his composure.

"Let's go down to the engine room," he said, leaning on the counter for support. "We put the grass down there to store it."

Since the engines had been constantly running to burn off the excess diesel, the engine room was exceedingly hot. And the bright green heap on the floor was smoking.

Spontaneous combustion was at work on the oil-rich plant material. There was a grey haze throughout the room, the fumes of which had permeated the rest of the ship.

All of a sudden they became very serious and the smouldering pot was quickly unloaded onto the dock. A small group of onlookers gathered to watch from the railings of the standing wharf above us. The skipper and his men went about their business with a crisp professionalism, despite the comments from the people at the railing. In a few minutes it was all on the dock, hosed down.

Once the danger to the boat was removed and the fire put out, the three RCMP members looked around them. They looked up at the faces on the railing. They looked at the pile of pot plants lying on the dock. They looked at one another. Then all three of them started to laugh again.

forty-four **DOUBLE-DOUBLE**

DOUBLE-DOUBLE ALWAYS STAYED at the Landing when he visited Stuart Island. It had much to do with the scenery. The incredible setting on the south end of the island gave a view all the way down Calm Passage as far as the north end of Cortes Island. Guests stayed in cabins spread out through the trees on a rocky hill overlooking the water. Double-Double always reserved one right on the cliff over the water's edge.

We had nicknamed him Double-Double after the size of the specially ordered rain gear he needed to wear. On the human scale of things, Double-Double was definitely a tyee. He weighed in at almost four hundred pounds. Whenever we went fishing together my boat took on a decided list. Whatever skinny little fishing partner he brought along, they just didn't have enough bulk to balance out the boat.

He was a man of immense appetites. Another reason he stayed at the Landing was the talent of the chef. As you can imagine, he liked to eat and eat well. He worked as a sales representative for one of the biggest food wholesalers in the US. He brought along extra supplies for his visits and the chef was always kept busy. No matter how much he had eaten before he got into my boat, he always brought along two coolers: one filled with beer, the other filled with candy, chocolate bars, and potato chips, in case we got hungry.

Of course, Double-Double was always the first one to reach for a cooler. He seemed always to be unwrapping something, so there was a constant flow of foodstuffs into his mouth. When we picked up our lines and travelled to another location, we departed in a cloud of candy wrappers that the wind blew out of the boat.

Double-Double was especially fond of a candy not available in the US that I had introduced to him, Mackintosh's Toffee. A thick bar of pure toffee, it became soft and difficult to divide in the hot weather. That was the reason for the other cooler. When the bar was kept cold, it was hard and brittle. I had shown him how to crack the bar by slamming it down on the gunnel of the boat. It had become one of our rituals. Double-Double punctuated his sentences with the slap of a toffee bar.

"You just can't find this stuff in Southern California," he told me once. "I guess it's too hot for it down there."

Double-Double also liked to tell jokes. Each time he came he had one in particular that would set the tone for the whole trip. This time it turned out to be a joke about stand-up comedians.

"Okay, Dave," he said to me, "I want you to ask me two questions. The first one is, 'What is the hardest job in the world?' The second is, 'Why is it so hard?' You got that?"

"What's the hardest job in the world?" I repeated.

"Being a stand-up comedian."

"Why is it so—"

"Timing!"

His partner this time was a business associate from Nebraska who had never been salmon fishing before. It was also his first visit to BC, and he was suitably impressed.

"Man, will you look at those eagles. Aren't they something? It's so beautiful up here, I don't care if I catch anything or not."

The two of them had been part of the group watching as the RCMP removed the smouldering pot from their engine room. The spectacle soon became a subject of conversation. Gord from Nebraska admitted he had never tried the stuff. Double-Double was staggered.

"What do you mean, you've never tried it? Didn't you ever go to college?"

"I went to college in Nebraska."

"So, what are you saying, they didn't have pot in Nebraska? I know that's bull, or were you just too much of a geek to know how to score?"

Double-Double cracked a Mackintosh's on the gunnel for emphasis.

"I'll bet Old Dave here could find us some. Hell, I bet Old Dave probably knows whose pot that was that got busted!"

"Old" Dave knew a number of things, chief among them the dangers of supplying illegal substances to guests.

forty-five **THE SONG OF JOY**

DOUBLE-DOUBLE COULD BE very persuasive. After all, he did make a very good living as a salesman. He was certainly his own best advertising. The next day I showed up with a small quantity of the substance, enough to keep them happy. (Double-Double didn't believe in delaying personal gratification. He wanted to try it immediately.)

We stopped by his cabin before we went fishing. Double-Double and I sat on the couch. Gord took a chair facing us, his back to the window and the view of the ocean. As the guide and person in charge of all the technical details, such as running the engines and baiting hooks, I was delegated to rolling the joint. Gord from Nebraska had a number of questions.

"So, what's this stuff going to do to me?"

"Quit worrying, will you? You're going to enjoy yourself," said Double-Double.

"How am I supposed to know when I'm stoned?"

"You'll know."

"Yeah, but how do you tell? What does it feel like?"

"You'll know."

"Does it happen all at once or does it come over you slowly?"

"You'll find out."

"It's not going to make me act weird or anything is it? I don't want to come to in my underpants lying in front of the lodge."

"You mean, like last year at the Christmas party when you

got so shit-faced you couldn't walk and woke up in the women's bathroom? Look, this stuff is different from booze. It's not going to make you act any stranger than you do already."

The discussion went back and forth between them while I concentrated on getting the joint rolled. As I worked, cleaning the grass of seeds and stems, I noticed, over Gord's shoulder, a sailboat rounding the point on its way to the Landing. I recognized it as a boat called *Song of Joy*. The guy who owned it operated a foundry. They worked with brass, making ornamental objects for homes and office interiors. As a hobby he made brass cannons. They were small but fully operational, definitely not toys. Many a sailboat captain from the eighteenth century would have been proud to have samples of his work on board.

He always saluted the lodge as he made his way to the dock. It added a little pomp and ceremony to his arrival.

I noticed some activity on the bow of the sailboat; I was well aware of the ritual that was taking place there. As I poured a small amount of grass onto the rolling paper, the men on the bow were pouring a small amount of powder into the muzzle of the cannon. I tamped down the grass carefully as they tamped the powder with a special ramrod. They rammed down the wadding, I rolled the paper between thumb and forefinger. I licked the gummed edge of the paper and sealed it as they placed a small fuse in the touchhole.

Gord was still talking.

"So, you're sure I'm going to know when this stuff's working and I'm not going to act weird behind it."

Double-Double was still murmuring his reassurances. He too had no idea that the *Song of Joy* was approaching or what it meant.

I struck a match to light the finished joint. On the boat out in the bay they prepared a long-handled "match" to light the fuse on the cannon. I took a few puffs to get the joint going properly and then passed it to Gord.

He held it very gingerly and took a small puff without inhaling. He looked as if he thought it might bite him.

"Oh come on, for pity's sake, just take a big haul and hold it in," Double-Double coached him.

Nebraska Gord shrugged his shoulders and took a long drag on the joint. He inhaled and held his breath.

At the same moment the *Song of Joy* let go with its cannon. I saw the smoke erupt out of the muzzle first and then heard an incredibly loud *boom!*

The windows of the cabin rattled and the whole building shook. Gord rocked forward from the force of the concussion. The blast rolled across the water and the echo reverberated off the mountains and around the resort. Still not looking behind him at the source of the detonation, Gord opened his eyes wide in amazement. They held a look of awe and childlike wonder. He let out his breath and looked instead at the joint in his hand.

forty-six **GIBBERISH**

THE HELICOPTER MADE a low pass over the landing pad at the Carringtons' resort. It circled as the pilot lined up his approach. Helicopters were quickly becoming the latest symbol of affluence at Stuart Island. At first only those owned by a big company made the occasional landing. They flew in busy executives to important meetings with clients. Then, last year, a couple of the opulent yachts showed up with a helicopter sitting on a specially modified pad atop their decks. That winter Troutbreath persuaded the Carringtons to install a landing pad on the front lawn. From the windows of the restaurant and lounge, people could be seen landing on it. It appealed to their clientele. It caught the crest of a trend. Soon they had private and personalized helicopters, like limousines, dropping off important-looking people in a windstorm of leaves and grass clippings.

A rumour had been circulated that a famous movie star was expected. People stopped to see who would be getting off. They peered out from the restaurant windows and stood in the lounge with drinks in their hands, watching. One man had brought a video camera. Down at the gas dock, where the rumour had originated, Troutbreath and I watched the landing with some amusement.

The helicopter, a brand new Bell Jet Ranger, hovered above the pad as it slowly descended. Its hull gleamed with new paint that matched the colour scheme on the Brelands' yacht. The landing gear settled on the pad, and the pilot shut down the engine. The rotors whined to a stop. The door opened. People craned their necks to get a better look; was it a movie star? A well-known athlete? A noted politician?

Wet Lenny stepped out of the helicopter and stood blinking in the bright sunlight. He held on to his baseball cap and ducked under the still spinning blades. The crowd noticed the tattered, blood encrusted sneakers and the Adidas bag, and there was a murmur of disappointment. The helicopter started up again and took off, leaving Lenny standing on the lawn in a swirl of leaves, alone.

Lenny was returning from the Brelands' estate, in time for the year-end salmon derby. It was an annual event that brought out the lodge's regular guests and a few select friends. A pool was established that provided for very substantial cash prizes. There was a prize for the biggest coho and one for the biggest fish overall. Some of the proceeds went to the community Salmon Enhancement program. The derby allowed people to drink expensive alcohol, smoke expensive cigars, catch fish, and still feel like they were doing something for the environment. It was a very popular event.

I talked with Wet Lenny while he was getting gas and bait for his boat. Some of his time in Vancouver had been spent with the FBI agent and the man from the SEC. I was curious to hear the outcome of their trip to Stuart Island.

"They had the co-operation of the Canadian authorities and they gave us an office where they could access the FBI's main computer database. They entered all the information in my notebooks to see if there were any correlations with the information they had."

"They entered all your notebooks?" I knew that Lenny's notes were substantial.

"Hey, these guys were experts, and they had scanning devices. You should have seen what they could do. They're very thorough."

"So, what did you find out?"

"They weren't at liberty to share that with me."

"Privileged information?"

"Yeah, I guess, something like that. But they did get very excited. So excited they let me have a favour."

"A favour?"

"See, they had all my information entered into their computer. It seemed the perfect time to ask it a question, the one I've been working on for years."

"In keeping with your line of research?"

"Exactly. I wanted to see if the computer could find any underlying patterns, some kind of unifying principle on the way fish are caught. I'd never have a better chance than with such a powerful computer system."

"I guess the FBI would have the best there is."

I should have thought about that last question more. Not that it was much of a question, but it was hardly out of my mouth and Lenny was into a long and excruciatingly detailed description of the kind of computer he'd had access to.

I finally had to interrupt him.

"What did you decide?"

Lenny looked a little glum as I put the question to him. He paused for a moment before he continued.

"Well, actually, it was disappointing. It was rather inconclusive. We asked the computer to find any one pattern that kept repeating itself. A common thread. The question itself was simple. Nothing happened for the longest time. Then the computer started to draw on the rest of the network. It called for more and more memory. It called up the memory from the other computers linked to the system. Computers in FBI offices all over the States started freezing up. It was kind of scary. It seemed almost to develop a mind of its own and was starting to take over. We finally had to force the program to shut down and withdraw the question."

"Were you able to get anything out of it at all?"

I knew how long Lenny had worked on this, how much time and energy he had expended on his quest.

"Well, there was something, just gibberish really."

"So, what was it?"

"We tried to warn the computer we were going to shut down the program if it took over other systems. We told it not to interfere with the other functions, to stop overriding other programs, or we would have to shut it down and go for lunch. That was when it gave us a printout. It made no sense at all and we hadn't even asked for it."

"Are you going to tell me what it said?"

"Like I said, it was really weird. It printed out the plans and specifications for the high-speed train that runs between Tokyo and Osaka. The one they call the Bullet Train."

I smiled inwardly and said aloud, "That's weird all right. What do you think it meant?"

"Like I said, it's just gibberish. It could have been from another file the agent was working on. Who knows? I do know we'll be seeing those guys again next summer."

"They're coming up here again? What the hell for?"

"There's a new case they're working on. Apparently, some time this summer a US customs officer was doing a routine check on an American businessman's luggage and found a document or papers of some sort that implicated him in selling secrets—industrial secrets—to the Russian government."

"What does that have to do with us up here?"

"The guy was on his way back from a fishing trip to the island when they found this stuff in his briefcase. He got really indignant, said he had never seen it before and didn't know where it came from. He created such a fuss that it only made them more suspicious. They did a complete body search, if you know what I mean. They got a translator in to read the document. It was written in Russian."

"I didn't realize we were becoming such a hub of international activity. You think those guys were just looking for an excuse to get back up here?"

"I think this is the last place those guys wanted to come back to. Thing is, I can't say as I blame them. I'm not planning on being here next summer."

"But Lenny, what are you going to do instead?"

Lenny became quiet and started to fiddle with his mustache. He mumbled something I didn't quite hear.

"Excuse me?"

"Mr. Breland offered me a job."

"A job? You're quitting? Won't you miss going fishing, Lenny?"

"I don't know, man, I'm not like you guys. I can't handle all this uncertainty. You and Vop and most of the other guides seem to revel in it. It drives me crazy."

"Nobody expects you to fish in the rapids, if that's what you mean. It scares the hell out of me most of the time."

"It's not that, even. I just can't go from day to day not knowing what's going to happen next. I get two guys in my boat looking at me expectantly. They want to catch fish, and I honestly can't tell them if we're going to catch a salmon, a cod, a dogfish, or even a twelve-inch LP record. I need something I can count on, where I can reasonably know what's going to happen next. I told Mr. Breland I would come and work for him."

It was sad, really, but I couldn't blame Lenny. Ever since humans climbed down out of the trees we've been looking for that kind of security—to be able to let go, to let down the guard for a time. It made me sad. I saw it as a source of much evil in the world, of mediocrity and sameness. It was the reason for "Weed Tree Eradication Programs." It was the reason for fast-food restaurants and strip malls, each one exactly the same as the other no surprises possible. The system designed for people who have become too timid to take a chance, to risk something and accept the consequences. Vop and the other guides were, unfortunately, an aberration. They were the exception that proved the rule.

Of course, I wasn't about to feel sorry for Wet Lenny. He was made for life.

 *forty-seven* **THE BLOOD KNOT**

THE DERBY WAS by invitation only and they didn't use any outside guides. That was the way the Carringtons wanted it, and not even Troutbreath could do anything about that. All the guides in the area wanted to get in on the sizable tips that came with winning the derby.

Vop and I didn't pay too much attention to what was going on; we were happy for the winners, but as independent guides we were excluded. There was no point in getting exercised over being left out. In the fishing holes we tried to stay out of the way of someone playing a big fish, but we did that anyway. One thing the derby did mean to us was the chance to use the laundry machines at the marina without having to wait in line.

On the last day of the event Vop collected all his dirty clothes for the purpose. It was before lunch and he had the laundromat to himself. He soon had all the machines working and wandered over to the lounge—a cold glass of beer would help pass the time waiting for the machines to finish. He got his beer and found a seat by an open window to enjoy a cool breeze.

He was engrossed in reading a two-year-old magazine when a face appeared in the window beside him. Vop was startled, and it took him a minute to recognize the face as belonging to Big Jake. Jake didn't look too good. Vop had seen dead cod floating past in the rapids that didn't look as bad. Jake's eyes bulged and lacked sparkle, his cheeks were puffy, and his lips looked like something found on the bottom of a herring pen.

"Jeez, Jake, you don't look so good."

"You should see what I look like from in here."

"Whatcha been doing to yourself?"

Jake burped and looked thoughtful; he was having a hard time forming words. His brain was occupied elsewhere.

"My guests and I caught the big fish yesterday." Big Jake burped again. He looked like a squid out of water. "We kind of partied it up last night. My guys were buying me drinks and then all the others started. It was just beer to begin with, then we switched to Scotch. Someone bought a round of sambuca and then they all started shooting tequila. After that I don't remember too good."

Jake's face worked. It had taken all his concentration to get the words out, now other areas of his body wanted his attention. A fierce internal struggle was being waged. He burped and made a face.

"You gotta go fishing for me this afternoon, I'm not going to make it. It's the last tide and I'm not even sure they'll want to go back out. They don't look much better than me. You'll get paid for four hours no matter what happens, and I'll give you a piece of my tip if we win."

"How big is your fish?"

Vop was thinking about clean laundry more than going fishing.

"It's just over twenty-eight pounds. The closest to it is only twenty-three."

The look of distress on Jake's face was intensifying.

"What kind of a tip are we talking about?"

Vop knew how to take advantage of the situation.

"They said they'd give me twenty percent."

Vop didn't look impressed.

Jake looked like something was welling up inside.

"I'll give you twenty-five percent of that."

Vop made a quick mental calculation. If these guys didn't go fishing, he stood to make four hours of guiding and twenty-five percent of a $2,000 tip just by saying yes.

Vop said yes.

Vop threw his clothes into the dryers and went back to the house to get some lunch. If he had to go fishing, he wanted to be ready. He organized his boat and took it over to the gas dock to fill up and get some bait. When he arrived, most of the resort boats had already left for the afternoon tide. One lone customer leaned against the wall of the gas shed, puffing on a large cigar. The weigh scale beside him was still set to the winning weight. The way he kept glancing at it, Vop guessed he must be one of Big Jake's fishing partners.

Vop went over and introduced himself.

"Yeah, Jake wanted me to take you guys out this afternoon. He wasn't feeling too well."

The man laughed. "You don't have to tell me. He was puking over the side all morning."

"Where's your partner?"

"I'm afraid he won't be coming with us either. After watching Big Jake he went off to do the same thing. The poor bastard couldn't even eat lunch."

The man was clearly enjoying their discomfort. He had the look of a more practised drinker.

"I've still got to get some gas and fill up my bait tank."

"Oh, take your time, take your time."

The man didn't seem to care if he ever left that spot or if the sun came up the next morning.

Vop busied himself with the gas and bait. He had a relaxed conversation with Troutbreath, who was watching the proceedings with immense delight. The man stood and smoked his cigar. Vop wondered if they would go out at all; the man seemed to be counting his winnings already. Vop could see himself spending the rest of the afternoon in the lounge. Then one of the other guide boats pulled into the dock.

As they tied up, the man with the cigar began giving them a hard time.

"You keeners didn't even come in for lunch. Were you stuck on the bottom the whole time?"

"We'll show you what the bottom looks like! We got you, you sonofabitch."

The men were red faced and beaming with excitement. They were both drinking beer and even the guide was smiling widely. He reached into the fish box and hauled out a large spring salmon. Its slab sides flashed silver and green. Its tail dragged on the dock as the guide carried it to the weigh scales. He dropped it on the hook and stepped back so Troutbreath could give it the official weigh-in. Troutbreath steadied the balance beam and adjusted the counterweight. He took his hands off the scale and watched intently as it settled.

"This is the bigger fish," he announced. "They've beaten you by half a pound."

The man took the cigar out of his mouth and inspected the scale closely. His demeanour underwent a transformation. He looked at his watch.

"What time is the derby officially over?" he asked Troutbreath.

"All the fish have to be weighed in by 5:30 to be legal."

Troutbreath was revelling in his official capacity.

The man looked at his watch again.

"Shit, are you finished screwing around?"

"I'm ready."

"Well, then, what are we doing standing around here? Let's go fishing."

Vop left the dock to the jeers of the man's rivals and steered the boat for the Second Hole. The flood tide was just starting to run, and they had learned from the guide that the fish had been caught there on the change. Even though the run out to the fishing hole was less than five minutes, the man chomped at his cigar, impatient the boat couldn't move any faster. He fretted while Vop baited his hook, and Vop had to remind him to let the line out slowly so it wouldn't get tangled on the way down.

I've always found it's impossible to hurry fishing. A fish will bite when it wants. There is nothing a person can do to make a fish pick up the pace. If there were, the guy in Vop's boat would have found it that afternoon. He chomped and fidgeted, reeled his line up and let it back down again. He reeled up so often Vop reminded him that the bait needed to be in the water to catch the fish.

Vop didn't want to say it out loud, but he was pessimistic about their chances. Twenty-eight pounds was tough to beat;

you don't catch fish that big on demand. However, the man's decline from cocky assurance to nervous insecurity was pitiful to watch. Vop wanted to reassure him. When the rod began to twitch Vop became more than usually excited.

"Hey, you're getting something!"

The man jerked the rod and began reeling so fast he scared off whatever it was and came up empty. Vop chided him about missing the strike as he put new bait on the line. The man watched from the edge of his seat, the cigar travelling from one side of his mouth to the other.

The fishing wasn't bad that afternoon. They watched as other boats went round the hole with a fish on or chased one out into the tide. The man would always inquire how big the fish was. If the boat went down the tide and didn't return, the cigar would get an extra workout.

After an hour on the water they hooked a big coho. It jumped several times and raced around the hole on top of the water. It tangled up with a couple of other guides and they spent precious minutes sorting out the snarled lines. When they finally got the fish to the side of the boat, the man, rather than being excited, was relieved to let it go and get back to fishing.

The good fishing attracted more boats and the hole became busy and chaotic. They had to get out of the way of the big fish being played past them, and Vop's guest was getting peevish about having to reel up all the time.

"Well, just try to put yourself in their place," Vop cajoled him, but it was like talking to a stump.

The rod tip jumped again. The fish on the line pulled hard and the man was immediately convinced he had the Big One. The fish took off across the hole. The guide beside them had to lift both his rods up in the air so Vop could duck under them as he steered. As they got past the guide, a tourist fishing in his own boat trolled over the man's fish. The man began shaking his fist and cursing. Vop took the rod out of his hands and passed it under one line, then cut off the other. The tourist shook his fist and cursed back at them.

Their fish headed directly for another guide who was also playing a salmon. He was tangled with Wet Lenny, who might have a fish of his own—the lines were so badly tangled it was hard to tell. All three boats came together in a jumble of lines, fishing rods, nets, and cursing guests. Vop backed the drag off on his reel so that the extra strain of the other lines wouldn't break off his fish.

A coho swam up beside Vop's boat and he quickly netted it and cut the line that trailed out of its mouth. He passed his rod to Wet Lenny, who managed to unwrap it from one of his guests' lines and pass the freed line back to Vop. Vop came out the other side of the mess with his fish still on. The man reeled in the line and the fish came to the side of the boat easily. The man looked down at it with obvious disappointment. It was not much more than twelve pounds.

They motored back to the other two boats in order to find the owner of the coho. Wet Lenny signalled it was his fish. He still had another fish wrapped up with the boat beside him, and was busy sorting out lines. Vop came up beside the other boat. He yelled to the guide to take the coho and flip it into Lenny's boat. Vop picked the fish up off the floor and held it in one hand while he steered with the other. The hooks had caught in the gills of the fish and blood poured out, making it even more slippery to handle. As the guide in the other boat reached out and took the fish by its tail, Vop noticed the woman in Wet Lenny's boat. She was an older woman and she was wearing a familiar-looking fluffy white angora sweater.

As the guide leaned into Wet Lenny's boat to drop the fish, a sudden surge of the tide caught the three boats. They lurched and clashed together. The guide momentarily lost his footing. The coho squirted out of his hands like a wet bar of soap. It landed with a slap high on the older woman's chest and slid down the length of the white sweater, leaving behind a thick smear of slimy red as it went. The surge pushed Vop away at the same time, and Lenny and Mr. Breland's mother were soon lost in the crowd of boats.

Time was running out and the man had chewed through his last cigar. The tide was at peak and the surges made it difficult to hold proper position. Vop had to start up his big motor at one point to power over the top of a boil that suddenly appeared in front of them. The man's line was caught by the foaming water, thrown to the surface, and dragged off by the tide. Vop had him reel in once more as he let the back eddy carry them toward the shore and into the calmer water of the Second Hole.

The outside of the back eddy was clogged with boats. Before Vop could start another pass down the rip, he had to wait for them to clear. Vop dropped a line in the shallow water while he waited. He wasn't expecting any result other than keeping his difficult customer occupied; then his guest's rod bounced once and pulled down hard.

Vop cursed, thinking a rock cod had come off the bottom and spoiled the bait. The line came to the surface of the water, running out taut across it. Drops of water glistened on the line like a string of pearls. Vop realized the fish had to be a salmon. He cursed again. It was going right for the kelp bed along the shore. He reached over and tightened the drag a little to put more pressure on the fish and slow it down. He steered the boat away from the shore and told the man to keep a steady pressure on the rod.

"It's just like turning a horse with a bit in its mouth," Vop said, hoping the man had gone horseback riding before.

The line curved and the fish turned back toward them. The man had to reel as fast as he could, taking in the slack line as it piled up in front of them. The fish passed under the boat. Vop grabbed the man and made him stuff the rod into the water almost as far as the reel, allowing the line to miss the propellers and engine shafts. While the man kept the rod in the water, Vop pivoted the boat around it. The fish was headed right for the pack of boats Vop had tried to avoid earlier.

Vop gunned the small engine and raced after the fish. He shouted and waved his free hand in the direction the fish was taking. The other guides understood immediately and moved out of the way. The same tourist, however, trolled blindly in front of them. The salmon went under the lines streaming off the back of the boat. Vop simply gathered them up like a sheaf of wheat in his arms.

A red-faced man in the stern of the tourist boat shouted angrily, "Hey, what the hell do you think you're doing?"

"I'm cutting your lines," Vop replied cheerfully.

His razor-sharp fish knife parted the lines, sending all their expensive gadgets and hardware to the bottom.

Once he got clear of the tourist, who was left sputtering impotently, Vop was on top of the pack of guide boats. He had to pass his rod under one guide's lines, but the rest were already reeling up and getting out of the way. Vop caught up to the fish that was now sitting on the bottom of the hole and sulking. All the guides cleared out a space for Vop to work the fish. He was sitting in the middle of an empty area with his rod bent straight down into the water.

Vop had the man lift up on the rod to try to move the fish off the bottom. Nothing happened. By steering into the current that swirled around them, Vop kept the boat over top of the fish. Vop checked the drag and tightened it just a little. The rod bent even farther into the water and still the fish didn't move. Vop tried hitting the butt of the rod with the palm of his hand. Sometimes the shock travelling down the taut line was enough to spook the fish into moving.

If the fish wouldn't run, there was no way to tire it out and the line could get snagged on the rocks on the bottom. Hitting the butt of the rod seemed to work. The fish began to move and the line started peeling out again. Vop turned to chase it and saw another tourist boat looming in front of him. It had floated into the clear section of the hole, the operator no doubt thinking it would be a good spot to fish, being empty of all the boats except one.

Vop waved at the tourists to move. They waved back.

Vop, caught up in the frenzy of the chase, screamed at them, "Hey, you morons, what the hell do you think I'm doing here? Reel in your lines!"

There were four morons in the small thirteen-foot Boston whaler. They all had a line in the water. They looked blankly at Vop as his boat came toward them, pushed by the crest of a surge. The fish circled their boat and came back toward Vop.

"Excuse me!" he yelled, trying not to lose control.

His guest lifted the rod to try to stay out of their way. For some unknown reason he also hit the freespool lever on the side of the reel.

"Don't touch that!" Vop yelled, horrified.

He reached out to flip it back in place, but he was too late. The reel exploded in a massive bird's nest.

"Oh shit! Oh shit!" the man observed helpfully.

Vop pulled his knife out and hacked at the tourists' lines. Each time he touched one, a rod on the other boat snapped straight. The tourists looked on incredulously. None of them wanted to say anything to the madman with the knife in his hand.

Vop's man started to pick at the mess of line surrounding his reel. Vop stopped him.

"Forget it, it's hopeless. I'll have to cut your line and splice it onto the other rod and reel."

"What do you mean, cut the line?"

"Do you want to argue? Or do you want to catch this fish?"

"What are you doing with that knife?"

"You're going to play the fish the old-fashioned way. By hand." Vop cut the line.

The man's mouth hung open. He couldn't believe Vop had just cut his own line. *Maybe he had gone out of his mind*, the man thought. Maybe ol' Vop here was having some sort of a breakdown. He still had a knife in his hand, though, and the man decided he didn't want to argue with him. He very much wanted to catch this fish.

"What am I supposed to do?"

"Watch."

Vop swung the boat around the tourists and left them staring at their empty rods. He gunned the motor after the fish.

"Haul the line in by hand, so the fish doesn't get any slack. Be careful how you bring it in. Let the line fall in coils onto the floor at your feet, but whatever you do—don't step on it. That's it, hand over hand. You don't need to be all that neat about how it coils. When you catch up to the fish, don't pull anymore, just keep tension on the line."

They passed the guides on the edge of the rip and followed the fish into the main channel. The man piled the line on the floor of the boat. His forehead was furrowed with concentration.

"Don't let your feet get tangled in the line," Vop warned him.

"I can feel it, the salmon, I can feel it pull. It's still there, the fish is still there."

"Whatever you do, don't jerk on the line, just keep it taut. If the fish runs, let the line slip through your fingers. Make the salmon earn the line but don't pull hard enough to break it. Don't forget, it's only twelve-pound test."

"How much is twelve pounds?"

"Not much!"

"Oww-ow-oooow...," said the man, "it's taking line."

"That's good."

"It's hurting my fingers."

"Isn't this great, just like in the good old days!"

Vop was already getting the other rod prepared. Letting the boat drift with the current, he stripped off the weight and leader.

"Ow-oww-owwooowww..."

Vop listened to the sound of the man's discomfort the same way he listened to the clicker on the reels. He could tell what the fish was doing by the sound.

A blood knot is used to join two similar pieces of monofilament. The knot is simple: one line is wrapped around the other and passed back through the beginning of those wraps. The other line is wrapped around the first, and the free end is passed back through the beginning of those wraps but in the opposite direction. The free ends are held, usually by the teeth, and the two lines are pulled to tighten the knot. If it is wrapped properly and the free ends don't pull out and lose the tension, it works; if not, you start again.

Vop tried not to notice the coils of line disappearing as he tied the knot. With both hands busy and the free ends in his teeth, he couldn't run the engine or steer the boat after the fish. The knot had to be finished before the line ran out. He worked quickly. The knot was the only one that would work in this situation, and he had to get it right. He took the two lines in either hand and pulled. The knot slipped and came loose. He had to tie it again.

"Keep the line tight on the fish. I've almost got the knot tied," Vop lied to the man. He turned the boat and took a little run toward the fish. The man gained more line back and piled it on the bottom of the boat. Vop tried to tie the knot again now that he had won some more time.

"It's running!" the man shouted.

Sweat was pouring down his face and he was slightly winded. Last night's activities where coming back to haunt him.

"Owww-ooooow-owowoow . . ."

The coils on the floor whipped off into the water. The line made a whispering sound as it ran. It hissed Vop's name over and over, teasing him.

"Vop—Vop—Vop—Vop . . ."

Vop concentrated on the knot. He knew this would be his last chance to get it right. The fish showed no signs of slowing down.

He wound the lines around each other. He passed the free ends through the eye of the knot, one on either side. He held them in his mouth. He pulled on both lines. The knot slipped again and came undone.

Vop took a deep breath. He had done this knot a thousand times. He had done it at home and he had done it while playing a fish the same way. He knew he wasn't paying it proper attention. The thought of the prize money was spoiling his focus. He grabbed the clippers and snipped off the now curled ends of the two lines. He sat down to start afresh.

"What are you doing?"

The man's eyes popped as he saw Vop sit down so casually. The boat bobbed up and down, spinning slowly as the current pushed it about. The man couldn't believe his eyes. Vop was actually smiling to himself. The line in the man's hand pulled and the fish ran again. He looked at his guide sitting down, fiddling with the line like some damn Sea Scout earning a merit badge.

Vop paid him no attention and didn't bother to answer. He was no longer on the boat. He was home on a rainy day, a fire burning in the wood stove, changing the line on his reels without a care in the world. He worked slowly and methodically.

"Oooooo-oo-ow—Oww-oww—OWWWWW…"

The coils were vanishing from the bottom of the boat.

"Vop—Vop—Vop—V-V-Vop—V-V-Vop…"

Vop finished wrapping the lines. The free ends were in his mouth. He pulled. The last coil shot out of the boat.

"Here!" Vop handed the man the other rod. "Start playing the fish with this one."

The line came up tight, the rod dipped, the knot held. They were playing the salmon on the end of a rod once more.

The boat had drifted a long way down the tide. The Second Hole was a tiny cluster of boats in the distance. The riptide off Kelsey Point was just ahead, and they still hadn't seen the fish. They avoided saying what was on both their minds.

Vop steered the boat to a calm place inside the point. The man worked the rod smoothly and gained his line back. The knot clicked through the eyes on the rod. The fish was coming to the surface, and the man was reeling in slack line.

"I can see the weight," he said after a few more minutes of quiet reeling.

Vop picked up the net and dipped it in the water. The weight came to the tip of the rod. Vop reached out with the net. The tired fish rolled on its side and Vop slipped the net over its head. As the fish hit the floor of the boat they both let out a whoop of relief and victory.

"What do you think?" said the man as he looked down at the fish.

"Man, it's going to be close, really close. It's long enough, but I can't tell if it's going to be thick enough."

The man looked at his watch.

"In another ten minutes it won't make any difference how thick it is."

Vop understood him immediately. Without cleaning the boat or putting the fish in the box, he started up the big motor and sped back to the lodge.

A crowd of people had gathered to await their return; word had spread quickly that they had left the Second Hole playing a big fish. Their exit from the fishing hole, after cutting every tourist's line, had made certain everyone noticed what was happening.

There was a collective intake of breath as the crowd saw the fish lying on the floor of the boat. Vop carried it over to the scales and dropped it on the hook. Troutbreath leaned in and squinted at the markings on the balance beam. He rubbed his chin and cleared his throat in an official manner. The counterweight was still set at the previous winning weight. The balance beam bobbed up and down. The crowd of people quieted as it slowed to a stop. The beam wasn't straight.

Troutbreath made the official announcement.

"It's the bigger fish by half a pound."

forty-eight **MAINTENANCE**

THE END OF the season at Stuart Island is a peculiar time. People keep disappearing. A guide or a member of shore staff, someone you've seen around and gotten to know on a casual basis, is suddenly not there anymore. One day they're carrying boxes at the company store or fishing beside you, the next day they simply vanish. It keeps on happening, like a strange horror movie. No one even comments on it. There is a slow whittling away, until there are only a handful of people left.

The same thing happens with the yachts. One by one they leave the docks and never return. Like the leaves on the maple trees, they fall off and disappear. The docks are left looking like empty branches awaiting the winter storms.

The activity around our house slacked off. It became peaceful; no helicopters or float planes taking off and landing; the number of outboards whining past greatly declined. The guides who used to come in and out, laughing and telling loud fish stories, had all disappeared.

Vop and Carol were off camping in Estero Basin. I decided to take advantage, in the best way possible, of the peace and quiet that had descended on the house and lay down on the couch to take a nap after lunch. I was just drifting off when there came a knock at the door.

"Hey, Brother Dave, are you in there?"

"Who is it?" I called out sleepily.

"It's me, Nelson."

"Oh, hey. Sorry, I was almost asleep here."

"I'm sorry, man, I didn't mean to disturb you, but I need some help with one of the eagles. I wonder if you can give me a hand?"

"Sure thing, that's no problem." I yawned sleepily and shook my head. "Don't mind me, I'll be with you in a minute."

I pulled on some warm clothes and my rain gear. A thick fog had rolled in that morning and the sun still hadn't burned it off. The far shore of the bay was hidden, and our voices and the sounds of the footsteps on the dock were muffled. No sooner were we away from the dock than we were closed in by fog. Though we were surrounded by land, all we could see was the water in front of us and the thick, white cloud all around.

We picked our way through the rapids and crossed the main channel in the direction of Nelson's resort. We went slowly and steered toward the unseen land with quiet certainty. The docks of his resort loomed suddenly and magically out of the fog.

He pulled up beside the outer finger. An aluminum ladder had been laid there, awaiting our arrival. In the filtered light of the fog, the ladder glowed. It looked Hamlet's father had used it to climb the walls of Elsinore Castle. We picked it up and laid it down the centre of the boat, the last few feet sticking out over the bow.

Once again we left the land behind and headed out into the blankness. Nelson made a few careful corrections to our course and a shoreline appeared before us. We ran along the shore for a distance and then Nelson picked a spot to land the boat. He ran it up onto a small gravel beach, the rocks sounding dully on the hull. We unloaded the ladder together.

We trudged along the fog-shrouded shore carrying the extension ladder between us. We conversed in hushed tones.

"So, Nelson, I've been meaning to ask you. What ever happened about the problem you were having with your eye?"

"You know, that was the strangest thing. My doctor in Campbell River couldn't figure it out, so he sent me to a specialist. They couldn't find anything obviously wrong either. It wasn't till just a couple of weeks ago, this specialist from Vancouver came to the River and I had an appointment with him. They were all there, my doctor, the specialist, the eye doctor from the big city, we even had a couple of other doctors who were just curious. They're all peering at me under a bright light with scopes and instruments. Then this specialist guy goes, 'Hmmmm...'—don't you hate it when a doctor goes 'Hmmmm...'? Then he puts something in my eye to freeze it up a little, gets this fine pair of tweezers out, and pulls a herring scale off my eyeball."

It took a moment to register the information.

"A what? Are you serious? A herring scale?"

"I swear, man, it was a fucking herring scale. You know how they get everywhere. I can see perfectly now."

"That's too weird."

"So I hear Vop won the big derby at the Carringtons'."

"And he's been impossible to live with ever since. Did you hear the size of the tip he got?"

"No, I just heard he'd won, eh."

"The guy was so happy he won back the biggest fish, he went nuts. He talked his partner, who'd slept through the whole afternoon, into splitting the prize money three ways. They didn't like awkward numbers, so rounded it up and gave Vop $3,500 dollars. By the time they'd partied it up all night Vop looked worse than Big Jake did the day before. He's gone off camping with Carol to recuperate."

"I hope they aren't sleeping under any trees."

"They're on the rocks in the middle of Estero Basin. The tallest tree is three feet high."

Nelson grunted his approval of Vop's choice. We cut away from the shoreline and into the trees that fringed it.

"How long do you think it will be before Wet Lenny marries the Brelands' daughter?" he asked.

"He's practically one of the family by now anyway. He's not guiding next year. Mr. Breland offered him a job."

"Well, that's fitting. It won't surprise me if he's running the company one day. He wouldn't be any worse than most of these guys we take fishing. I wouldn't trust most of them to organize my tackle box. Here's the tree up ahead."

We leaned the ladder against the trunk of the tree. The

eagle was in the branches not far above us. Nelson hauled on the rope to raise the extension until the ladder was resting on the branch beside it.

Nelson paused before he climbed. Floating in the rapids in a Santa Claus suit waiting to die of hypothermia had given him a more philosophical turn.

"Some people might envy him, but I feel sorry for the poor bastard. Give him another twenty years and he'll be just like Herbert Crane and the rest of them. He won't know his own children or his wife—hell, he won't even be able to find his ass if you gave him the charts and a compass.

"I know people who believe a shadowy cabal of cigar-smoking men runs the world, holding private meetings in mahogany-panelled rooms to decide the fate of the world. I wish I could believe in that too . . . I could sleep at night! It's a much simpler world. All we'd have to do is get rid of those men and you could change things for the better. It would all be so easy. But it isn't like that at all, and that scares the hell out of me.

"It's like we're on this huge ocean liner. A big luxury cruise ship, you know? The wind's starting to blow and the seas are kicking up. Waves are crashing against the hull and it looks like we're getting too close to those rocks up ahead. The passengers complain most of the time anyway, but now they're really getting upset. The boat is rocking too much. It's affecting the enjoyment of the cruise. They can't play shuffleboard. Only a few of them even notice the reef, and they just expect the people on the bridge to take care of things . . . But you and me, we've been up on the bridge and the only people there are a couple of dipshits like us doing maintenance! Mopping the floor and polishing the binnacle with a white cloth . . . the ship's going down, but at least it'll look good while it sinks."

Nelson climbed the ladder. As he reached the branch where the eagle sat, it turned its head toward him. There was a mechanical whir and it stretched out its wings. Its head turned in the other direction and it started to make its strange, high-pitched, wickering cry. Then the head stopped abruptly. The eagle kept wickering the same note over and over as its head went back and forth. Then there was a metallic click and the head turned back to the starting point. There was another whirring sound and the wings came back down. Before it could start another cycle Nelson reached out to a plastic box at the bird's feet.

"You know, those old-fashioned eagles may have been nothing but flea-ridden scavengers, but at least they didn't take this much damn maintenance," he called out to me over his shoulder.

Nelson took hold of the knob on the front of the box and turned it to OFF.

AUTHOR'S NOTE

WHEN I LEARNED not too long ago that "creative non-fiction" was a writing category, I thought it was the perfect description for fishing stories. Now, such stories are perceived as tall tales in which the fish grow bigger after they are dead, but that is not the case. Among fishing guides there is an unspoken understanding that we always tell the truth when it comes to the size of the fish, and that is what I have done. That part is the non-fiction. I had to get creative with all the rest. Dates, places, people, all were treated with a certain artistic license. Three or four people might be combined into one character. Events that took place over several seasons were condensed into one summer. Liberties were taken. In fact, after careful consideration, I had to tone down some of the stories—if the real truth came out, people wouldn't believe it. Skepticism might creep in and undermine the non-fiction part. I didn't want that; my reputation as a guide might come into question.

ACKNOWLEDGEMENTS

THIS BOOK IS for Kim—without her love, support, and encouragement, it would never have been written.

I want to thank Ruth for letting me be "that guy," and Jamie for his help with some of the technical details.

I also want to thank Roger, Jim, Mike, Tommy, Nick and Henry, Rob, Bob, Helene, Donna, Heidi, Dahl, Jode, Keith, and all the other Stuart Island guides who helped make me a better fisherman.

KIMBERLY DENNESS-THOMAS

ABOUT THE AUTHOR

DAVID GIBLIN was born in Norwich, Norfolk, England. His father, a merchant seaman, ran away to sea at the age of sixteen and worked on the North Sea on a Norfolk sail-powered fishing boat, and later on freighters that visited Vancouver and Port Alberni. In 1957, when David was six weeks shy of his sixth birthday, his family moved to Canada. He grew up in Horseshoe Bay, on Vancouver's North Shore, and began messing around in small boats early on. In the '70s, while living on Cortes Island, he heard about Stuart Island from a neighbour who worked as a cook at Big Bay Marina. He did his rookie year there before getting his own boat and going independent. He worked as a guide for fifteen years, the last five as head guide at Stuart Island Resort. This book grew out of the stories the guides would tell. As an unpublished manuscript, *The Codfish Dream* was a finalist in the Cedric Literary Awards in the creative non-fiction category. David studied art at the University of British Columbia; Kootenay School of the Arts (now Selkirk College); Capilano College (now University), with Allen Wood; and Victoria College of Art, under Jim Gordaneer and Bill Porteus. He lives in Cobble Hill, BC.